AAT

LEVEL 1 AWARD IN BUSINESS SKILLS
LEVEL 1

Workbook

2022 Edition

For assessments from September 2022

Second edition 2022
ISBN 9781 5097 4631 6
British Library Cataloguing-in-Publication Data
A catalogue record for this book is available from the British Library

Published by
BPP Learning Media Ltd
BPP House
Aldine Place
London
W12 8AA

www.bpp.com/learningmedia

Printed in the United Kingdom

> Your learning materials, published by BPP Learning Media Ltd, are printed on paper obtained from traceable sustainable sources.

All our rights reserved. No part of this publication may be reproduced, stored in a retrieval system or transmitted, in any form or by any means, electronic, mechanical, photocopying, recording or otherwise, without the prior written permission of BPP Learning Media Ltd.

The contents of this book are intended as a guide and not professional advice. Although every effort has been made to ensure that the contents of this book are correct at the time of going to press, BPP Learning Media makes no warranty that the information in this book is accurate or complete and accepts no liability for any loss or damage suffered by any person acting or refraining from acting as a result of the material in this book.

We are grateful to the AAT for permission to reproduce the sample assessment(s). The answers to the sample assessment(s) have been published by the AAT. All other answers have been prepared by BPP Learning Media Ltd.

©
BPP Learning Media Ltd
2022

A note about copyright

Dear Customer

What does the little © mean and why does it matter?

Your market-leading BPP books, course materials and e-learning materials do not write and update themselves. People write them on their own behalf or as employees of an organisation that invests in this activity. Copyright law protects their livelihoods. It does so by creating rights over the use of the content.

Breach of copyright is a form of theft – as well as being a criminal offence in some jurisdictions, it is potentially a serious breach of professional ethics.

With current technology, things might seem a bit hazy but, basically, without the express permission of BPP Learning Media:

- Photocopying our materials is a breach of copyright

- Scanning, ripcasting or conversion of our digital materials into different file formats, uploading them to social media or e-mailing them to a third party is a breach of copyright

You can, of course, sell your books, in the form in which you have bought them – once you have finished with them. (Is this fair to your fellow students? We update for a reason.) Please note the e-products are sold on a single user licence basis: we do not supply 'unlock' codes to people who have bought them secondhand.

And what about outside the UK? BPP Learning Media strives to make our materials available at prices students can afford by local printing arrangements, pricing policies and partnerships which are clearly listed on our website. A tiny minority ignore this and indulge in criminal activity by illegally photocopying our material or supporting organisations that do. If they act illegally and unethically in one area, can you really trust them?

Contents

		Page
Qualification purpose and structure		v
Assessment strategy for Business Skills unit assessment		xviii
1	Working in the business environment	1
2	Working in the business environment: Test your learning	51
3	Using numbers in business	61
4	Using numbers in business: Test your learning	89
Chapter tasks: answers		97
Test your learning: answers		107
BPP practice assessment 1		117
BPP practice assessment 1: answers		127
BPP practice assessment 2		135
BPP practice assessment 2: answers		147
Index		157

How to use this Workbook

This Workbook for the Level 1 Award in Business Skills has been written specifically to ensure comprehensive yet concise coverage of the assessment criteria. It is fully up to date as at June 2022 and reflects both the AAT's study guide and the practice assessments provided by the AAT.

This Workbook contains odd-numbered chapters containing the learning you need to do to prepare yourself for the assessment, and even-numbered chapters giving you assessment practice in the form of assessment style tasks.

You should work through the book taking each chapter in turn, working through the information presented to you and then attempting the tasks given. You can compare your answers with the answers given towards the back of the Workbook. If you have struggled with any tasks, look back at the learning chapter to see where you have gone wrong. At the end of the Workbook there are two assessment-standard practice assessments prepared by BPP for you to work through. You should not attempt these until you have tried all the tasks in the even-numbered chapters. These practice assessments have answers so that you can judge how you are doing once you have completed them.

If you have any comments about this book, please use the review form at the back.

Qualification purpose and structure

The **Level 1 Award in Business Skills** covers a range of skills and the relevant supporting knowledge in two mandatory units:

- Level 1 Working in the business environment
- Level 1 Using numbers in business

The qualification is assessed in one end-of-qualification assessment (see 'Assessment strategy' section below for more detail).

Students completing this qualification will develop an understanding of how different organisations operate, across both the public and private sectors. They will learn how to contribute effectively in the workplace by working with others, managing their time, behaving professionally and maintaining security of data. Students will also gain an understanding of the ways in which businesses process sales and purchases and the documentation and procedures used to move goods and services between businesses.

Studying this qualification will also equip students with the basic numerical skills needed in the workplace, and in life outside work. These numerical skills range from simple calculations that are used most often in business to working with decimals, percentages and fractions, and applying proportions and ratios. Students will also learn tools and techniques to enhance the presentation of numerical data.

This qualification will not include learning outcomes on being able to apply for a job, including interview preparation. We will be exploring with our learning services team what optional supporting resources on these topics can be made available to students on the lifelong learning portal.

Working in the business environment

Learning outcomes

1. Develop skills for the workplace
2. Understand how organisations operate
3. Understand how sales and purchases support businesses
4. Apply business procedures to sales and purchases

Scope of content

This section illustrates the depth and breadth of content to be delivered for this unit. All areas indicated in the table below must be covered in teaching.

Learners may not be assessed on all content, or on the full depth or breadth of a piece of content. Content assessed may change over time to ensure validity of assessment.

1. Develop skills for the workplace

1.1 The responsibilities of the employee and employer

Learners need to understand:

1.1.1 the responsibilities of the employee:
- follow workplace policies and procedures
- report any health and safety risks

1.1.2 the responsibilities of the employer:
- provide induction to new staff that includes organisation policies and procedures
- provide a safe working environment.

1.2 Working and communicating with others

Learners need to understand:

1.2.1 the characteristics of effective team working:
- clear roles and responsibilities
- respect
- trust
- co-operation
- common goals
- realistic deadlines
- good communication
- timekeeping
- reliability
- professionalism

1.2.2 the benefit of working in teams:
- collaboration
- sharing ideas
- team morale
- achieving goals
- utilising individuals' skills and expertise
- shared learning

1.2.3 why different methods of communication are used in the workplace:
- emails
- online meetings
- reports
- spreadsheets
- telephone calls
- face-to-face
- hybrid working
- instant messaging
- intranet
- shared communication channels

1.2.4 how software is used in workplace communications:
- word processing
- spreadsheet
- email
- presentation.

1.3 Time management

Learners need to know:

1.3.1 how to use planning aids to manage their time:
- online (calendars)
- work schedules
- online collaboration
- to-do lists (including digital to-do-lists)

1.3.2 the effect on others of failing to meet a deadline:
- others may be relying on work produced by the team
- impact on other deadlines of the team

1.3.3 that work might be allocated based on how urgent and important it is.

1.4	**Professional behaviour**

Learners need to understand:

1.4.1 the principle of confidentiality:

- Compliance with General Data Protection Regulations

1.4.2 how to follow policies and procedures:

- sustainability (environmental awareness)
- use of social media
- use of personal phones
- dress codes
- answering and making business phone calls

1.4.3 principles of good time keeping:

- being at work on time
- keeping to break times
- not leaving early
- discussing workloads with supervisor

1.4.4 principles of polite communication with colleagues and customers:

- using correct names
- listening to the other person
- avoiding slang, swearing and offensive humour

1.4.5 personal qualities required for employment:

- honesty
- adaptability
- trustworthiness
- commitment.

1.5	**Understand the importance of keeping data and information secure**

Learners need to understand:

1.5.1 why it is important to make sure that data and information is secure:

- prevents loss and unauthorised sharing of information
- protects against computer failure or viruses
- maintains confidentiality
- protects customer information
- complies with any legal requirements
- loss of business / personal reputation

1.5.2 how data and information is kept secure:
- use of strong passwords / not sharing passwords
- screensavers
- encryption
- firewalls
- use of secure network: remote / hybrid working
- storage of hard-copy records, physical access restrictions
- storage of soft-copy records: cloud-storage, archives, secure back-ups, restricted access, cybersecurity
- authentication required to access cloud-based information
- not sharing laptops/computers with others
- not leaving confidential information where non-authorised personnel may see/not working in a public space
- not discussing confidential information where non-authorised personnel may hear
- anti-virus software
- cookies and privacy settings
- the importance of only sharing information with authorised personnel
- checking correct recipient before sending required information

1.5.3 threats to data security:
- viruses
- hacking
- phishing
- system crashes
- employee fraud
- corrupt files
- natural disasters
- accidental deletion.

2. Understand how organisations operate

2.1 Key features of different sectors

Learners need to know:

2.1.1 the key features of the retail sector:
- sells goods to the public
- may have a number of branches, franchises or online

2.1.2 the key features of the manufacturing sector:
- makes products either for sale or as components for further manufacturing

2.1.3 the key features of the service sector:
- provides services rather than manufacturing or selling goods

2.1.4 the key features of the charity and voluntary sector:
- generates income to support its purpose

2.1.5 the key features of the public sector:
- provides services to the public
- funded by government

2.1.6 businesses can operate from a physical location and/or online.

2.2 Purpose of different types of organisations

Learners need to understand:

2.2.1 that some organisations are run for profit:
- sole trader
- partnership
- private limited company (Ltd)
- public limited company (PLC)

2.2.2 that some organisations are run not for-profit:
- charities
- community and voluntary organisations
- public sector
- social enterprises
- community interest companies (CICs)

2.2.3 additional considerations:
- sustainability
- ethics
- diversity and equal opportunities.

2.3	**Structure of organisations**
	Learners need to understand:
2.3.1	different organisations of different sizes have different structures
2.3.2	typical departments within an organisation and what they do:
	– finance
	– human resources
	– information technology
	– sales and marketing
	– production
	– distribution
2.3.3	the structure of a three-level organisation chart:
	– department staff
	– department managers
	– directors
2.3.4	levels of responsibility in an organisation and who each level reports to:
	– staff
	– manager
	– director.

3. Understand how sales and purchases support businesses

3.1	**Purpose of sales and purchases**
	Learners need to understand:
3.1.1	the importance of sales and purchases:
	– businesses need money to operate
	– selling goods and services makes money (income)
	– buying goods and services costs money (expenses)
	– businesses need more income than expenses to run profitably
	– the meaning of profit and loss: income minus expenses
	– the meaning of surplus and deficit for not-for-profit organisations
3.1.2	possible problems when there is more expenditure than income:
	– not enough money to pay for expenses and purchases
	– bank account may become overdrawn
	– suppliers may withdraw credit
	– business could fail
3.1.3	possible opportunities when there is more income than expenditure:
	– saving opportunity
	– business growth
	– repay loans
	– provide return to owners.
	Exclusion: distinction between gross profit and net profit.

3.2	**Principles of sales**	
	Learners need to understand:	
	3.2.1	who goods or services are sold to: – customers – clients
	3.2.2	that some sales are made on a cash basis
	3.2.3	that some sales are made on a credit basis.
	Exclusion: returned goods.	
3.3	**Principles of purchases**	
	Learners need to understand:	
	3.3.1	who goods or services are bought from: suppliers
	3.3.2	that some purchases are made on a cash basis
	3.3.3	that some purchases are made on a credit basis
	3.3.4	that businesses may have a list of approved suppliers.
	Exclusion: returned goods.	
3.4	**Payment terms**	
	Learners need to understand:	
	3.4.1	the purpose of payment terms: – to ensure that customers know when to pay their invoices – to ensure that suppliers are paid at the agreed time
	3.4.2	common terminology: – payment in advance – payment on delivery – payment 10, 14, 30 or 60 days after invoice date – payment at end of the month of invoice
	3.4.3	how payment terms offered to customers/clients and received from suppliers affect the bank balance.

4. Apply business procedures to sales and purchases

4.1	**Importance of business procedures**	
	Learners need to understand:	
	4.1.1	why it is important to follow business procedures: – to avoid errors – to avoid missing internal and external deadlines – to ensure processes are completed as required by the business – to maintain good business relationships with customers and suppliers

4.1.2 how to follow procedures:
- completing documents fully and accurately
- completing documents on time
- obtaining authorisation.

4.2 Business procedures for sales

Learners need to understand:

4.2.1 documents used in the sales process:
- customer order
- delivery note
- sales invoice

4.2.2 the process of making sales:
- customer places order
- business delivers goods or provides services to customer
- business invoices for goods or services
- business receives and records the income.

4.3 Business procedures for purchases and expenses

Learners need to understand:

4.3.1 documents used in the purchases and expenses process:
- approved supplier list
- purchase order
- delivery note
- goods received note (GRN)
- purchase invoice

4.3.2 the process of purchasing goods or services:
- business selects supplier
- business raises purchase order
- business receives goods or services from supplier
- business checks delivery note against goods received
- business completes goods received note (GRN)
- business makes a note of any differences and queries them with supplier
- business checks purchase invoice against purchase order and delivery note/ goods received note (GRN)
- business makes payment and records the expenditure.

4.4 Procedures

Learners need to be able to:

4.4.1 select an approved supplier for specified goods or services

4.4.2 check for differences between documents in the purchase process (purchase order, goods received note (GRN), delivery note):
- incorrect items or quantity of goods
- items missing from delivery
- incorrect item price
- incorrect calculations.

Using numbers in business

Learning outcomes
1. Perform simple business calculations
2. Calculate decimals, fractions, percentages, proportions and ratios
3. Use tools and techniques to present numerical data

Scope of content

This section illustrates the depth and breadth of content to be delivered for this unit. All areas indicated in the table below must be covered in teaching.

Learners may not be assessed on all content, or on the full depth or breadth of a piece of content. Content assessed may change over time to ensure validity of assessment.

1. Perform simple business calculations

1.1 Record and sort whole numbers

Learners need to be able to:

1.1.1 record numbers in words and figures

1.1.2 arrange numbers, including positive and negative numbers, in ascending and descending order
- identify highest number
- identify lowest number

1.1.3 calculate range

1.1.4 identify most frequently occurring number or numbers (mode).

1.2 Check results of calculations

Learners need to be able to:

1.2.1 estimate figures

1.2.2 round figures:
- to whole numbers
- to one/two decimal places

1.2.3 estimate highest and lowest possible results

1.2.4 cross-check calculations.

1.3 Identify differences between figures over time

Learners need to be able to:

1.3.1 identify increases

1.3.2 identify decreases.

1.4 Complete calculations

Learners need to be able to:

1.4.1 use numerical functions:
- addition
- subtraction
- multiplication
- division
- calculate average (mean)

1.4.2 work with common units of time:
- hours
- days
- weeks
- months
- quarters
- years.

2. Calculate decimals, fractions, percentages, proportions and ratios

2.1 Calculate decimals, fractions and percentages of numbers

Learners need to be able to:

2.1.1 calculate decimals

2.1.2 calculate simple fractions:
- 1/2
- 1/4
- 1/5
- 1/10

2.1.3 calculate whole percentages

2.1.4 calculate figures using whole percentages

2.1.5 express a number as a fraction or percentage of another.

2.2 Calculate equivalent fractions, percentages and decimals

Learners need to be able to:

2.2.1 convert fractions into percentages and decimals

2.2.2 convert percentages into fractions and decimals

2.2.3 convert decimals into percentages and fractions.

2.3 Calculate and apply simple proportions and ratios

Learners need to be able to:

2.3.1 express one number as a proportion of another

2.3.2 express two numbers as a ratio

2.3.3 apply a proportion or ratio to a number.

3. Use tools and techniques to present numerical data

3.1 Formulas

Learners need to be able to:

3.1.1 use formulas when completing calculations:
- addition
- subtraction
- multiplication
- division.

3.2 Formatting

Learners need to be able to:

3.2.1 use formatting to enhance presentation of information:
- bold
- italics
- underline
- change font colour / size
- fill cell
- accounting
- thousands
- percentages
- decimal places.

Assessment strategy for Business Skills unit assessment

There will not be a separate Qualification Technical Information (QTI) document for this assessment.

Assessment method	Marking type	Duration (suggested)
Computer based assessment	Computer marked	1 hour 30 minutes

Learning outcomes	Weighting
Working in the business environment	
1. Develop skills for the workplace	10%
2. Understand how organisations operate	20%
3. Understand how sales and purchases support businesses	15%
4. Apply business procedures to sales and purchases	15%
Using numbers in business	
1. Perform simple business calculations	15%
2. Calculate decimals, fractions, percentages, proportions and ratios	15%
3. Use tools and techniques to present numerical data	10%
Total	**100%**

1 Working in the business environment

Chapter coverage

This chapter introduces the types of organisations you may encounter and describes the way that they are typically structured. It also covers skills that are required to be effective in the workplace and provides information about how sales and purchases support a business.

	Section number
How organisations operate	1
Developing workplace skills	2
How sales and purchases support businesses	3
Sales and purchase procedures	4

1 How organisations operate

Organisations may have a number of different purposes.

Commercial organisations aim to make a profit, usually by selling goods or providing services and are often referred to as businesses.

You may come across other types of organisation that do not seek to make a profit. These include government bodies whose purpose is to maximise service delivery to the public.

We can categorise an organisation by whether it is run for profit or not run for profit.

Organisations run for profit

This type of organisation, referred to as businesses, can take a number of forms dependent upon their ownership structure. The simplest form is a sole trader.

A **sole trader** is a business owned and run by an individual and there is no legal distinction between the business and the individual. Small service businesses, such as plumbers and electricians are often sole traders.

Partnerships are businesses owned and run by a number of individuals. Professional firms such as lawyers or accountants are often formed as partnerships. There are a number of different organisation types within each category as shown below. As with sole traders, there is no legal distinction between a partnership and the partners who own it.

A **limited company** is a separate legal entity from those who own it. Limited companies are owned by the shareholders who are not necessarily involved in running it. Shareholders appoint the board of directors who run the company.

Private limited company (Ltd) is a form of limited company that cannot sell its shares to the general public.

Public limited company (PLC) is a form of limited company that can sell its shares to the public, for example through a stock market.

How it works

The table below shows the different types of organisation that are run for profit:

Sole traders	Owned and run by an individual
Partnerships	Owned and run by a number of individuals
Limited companies (private or public)	Owned by shareholders, run by directors

KEYWORDS

A **sole trader** is a small business run and owned by an individual.

A **partnership** is a business owned and run by a number of individuals.

A **limited company** is owned by shareholders and run by directors. Some companies are very large.

Private limited company (Ltd) is a form of limited company that cannot sell its shares to the general public.

Public limited company (PLC) is a form of limited company that can sell its shares to the public, for example through a stock market.

Organisations not run for profit

There are also organisations with different aims. These fall into five main categories.

Public sector organisations are funded by government and their aim is typically to maximise service delivery to the public or achieve an objective of government such as collecting taxes. Examples of public sector bodies include the Crown Prosecution Service, HM Revenue and Customs and the National Health Service (NHS).

Charities aim to raise money from the public which they spend in order to further their specified purpose. Some of the largest charities in the UK are Oxfam, the Arts Council of England and Cancer Research UK. Charities must be run in accordance with specific charities legislation.

Community and **voluntary organisations** raise money to perform a service in their local area, for example foodbanks. They are not run to make a profit.

Social enterprises are non-profit-making organisations that invest or donate the money raised to create positive social and environmental change. These organisations support people through employment and help transform communities. Examples include the Big Issue and Eden Project.

Community Interest Companies (CICs) are a special form of company for use by 'social' enterprises pursuing purposes that are beneficial to the community, rather than the maximisation of profit for the benefit of owners

How it works

The table below shows the different types of organisation that are not run for profit:

Public sector	Government funded	Service delivery to the public or achieve government objective
Charities	Funded by the public	Support specified purpose
Community and voluntary organisations	Funded by the public	Support specified purpose
Social enterprises	Funded by profit	Creation of positive social and environmental change
Community Interest Companies (CICs)	Funded by profit	Benefits for the community

Other considerations

Sustainability, ethics and diversity and equal opportunities are relevant to business organisations.

Sustainability concerns meeting our own needs for today, but not at the expense of future generations. Resources should only be used at a rate they can be replaced. Organisations are expected to act sustainably by the public, but currently there is no legal obligation from them to do so.

Ethics are a moral guide to behaviour. They form from the values of the culture we live in, but individuals decide what right and wrong means to them. Business ethics concerns the values that businesses have. They will form policies and procedures to enable them to embody these values.

Diversity and equal opportunities means that organisations should employ people with as wide a range of backgrounds as possible (for example, culture, race, sex and age) and provide the same employment opportunities and benefits to all.

KEYWORDS

Organisations in the **public sector** are funded by governments to deliver services or achieve government aims.

Charities raise money in order to spend it on a specified purpose.

Community and voluntary organisations raise money to perform a service in their local area.

Social enterprises are run like profit-making organisations but invest or donate the money raised to create positive social and environmental change.

Community Interest Companies (CICs) are a special form of company for use by 'social' enterprises pursuing purposes that are beneficial to the community.

Sustainability concerns meeting our own needs for today, but not at the expense of future generations.

Ethics are a moral guide to behaviour.

Diversity and equal opportunities means that organisations should employ people with as wide a range of backgrounds as possible and treat them the same.

Sectors

We can also categorise organisations by sector. This looks at the nature of the organisation's main activities. We have just looked at two of these: charities and the public sector. Organisations run for profit (ie businesses) can be involved in a range of commercial activities. Businesses often have a **physical location** (such as an office or factory), but they can also operate entirely **online** as well.

How it works

The table below shows the different sectors organisations may fall into:

Sector	Features	Examples
Retail	Sell goods to the public	Tesco
	May operate through physical branches or franchises	M&S
		McDonalds (franchise)
	May also operate online	
Manufacturing	Produce finished goods or components for further manufacturing	Rolls Royce
		Unilever
Services	Provide services	HSBC
	Customers may be the public or other organisations	Aviva
Public sector	Service delivery to the public or achieve government objective	Police service
		NHS
	Funded by government	
Charity and voluntary	Income supports specified purpose	Oxfam
		Save the Children

At this stage of your studies, you do not need to know anything more about these types of organisation, only the sectors they are in and the main purpose of organisations in those sectors.

TASK 1 Sector classification

For each of the following businesses, select the sector that they operate in.

A travel agent

A maker of musical instruments

An online bookseller

Options:

Manufacturing
Public sector
Retail
Services

Organisational structure

The **size of an organisation** will influence how it is structured (or organised).

A sole trader such as an electrician may just be one person without any employees. That person will provide the service as an electrician, but on top of this will have to do many other tasks associated with a business, such as answer the phone, prepare and send out quotations, prepare and send invoices, maintain accounting records, organise advertising etc.

As organisations get larger they are typically split into departments, each handling a different part of the organisation's workload. This approach allows staff members to specialise in particular tasks for increased efficiency.

Exam Focus Point

A previous Examiner Report stated that students often struggled to explain what an organisation chart was and what it is used for. Ensure that you understand that there are different departments within a business, and that there will be key tasks assigned to those departments, for example, the payment of suppliers will be assigned to the Accounts Payable department.

Departmental structure

The table below describes typical departments in an organisation and what they do.

Department	Responsibilities
Production	Ensuring that raw materials are made into finished goods efficiently. They may work with the finance department and/or procurement (in larger companies, this is a department that is responsible for buying in materials) to ensure that they have the correct materials ordered in on a timely basis.
Distribution (despatch)	Getting goods to the customer, including packaging and delivery. They will interact with the finance department (to let them know that invoices will need raising for goods recently despatched) and the sales department (to get the details of where the goods will go).
Finance	The capture and use of financial information, including the preparation of accounting information. They will work with several other departments to ensure they have all the financial information.
Sales and marketing	Advertising, promotion and public relations, together with interactions with customers (such as through social media channels).
Information technology (IT)	Operating and supporting technology systems and ensuring that they assist an organisation in meeting its objectives.
Human resources	Managing an organisation's staff including recruitment, legal compliance, training and compensation. They are often involved with the payroll (although this may be assigned to the Finance Department).

The size of each department will be affected by the size of the organisation. For example, the finance department of a small sole trader may just be a single accountant, whereas a very large company might employ several hundred people in this department. It will also be related to the sector in which it operates. For example a service sector organisation such as a partnership of lawyers would not need a production department.

Some departments such as despatch and sales and marketing are focused on servicing customer needs, whereas others, such as human resources and IT, are more internally focused and meet the needs of other departments.

TASK 2 Which departments would be responsible for the following tasks at an organisation?

Ensuring the manufacturing process within a factory is maintained

Producing an employment contract for new staff

Producing financial plans for management

Options:

Finance
Human resources
Information and communication technology
Production

Organisational reporting lines

As organisations get larger it is important that they are well organised. It is essential that all employees know what their role is and who they report to.

The structure of who members of staff report to is referred to as an organisation's reporting lines. If you report to someone they are responsible for setting your objectives and goals and evaluating your performance. They are also the primary person to whom you should raise issues related to your employment functions.

How it works

Those working in an organisation can be put into three levels.

	Responsibility	Reports to
Directors	Formulating business objectives and strategy to achieve them	Shareholders (owners)
Managers	Day-to-day management consistent with strategy and objectives	Director responsible for that department
Staff	Performing departmental function assigned to them	Department manager

Reporting lines in a large organisation are usually based on departments. For example, a bookkeeper working in the finance department would report to the finance manager, who would in turn report to the organisation's finance director.

In a really large organisation there could be many other stages in reporting lines such as junior managers reporting to senior managers.

The structure of an organisation can be thought of as a pyramid with more individuals making up each level as you go down. Below is an example of an organisation chart. This is a simple one which shows the key department managers and how they report to the managing director, together with the departments and staff that they are responsible for.

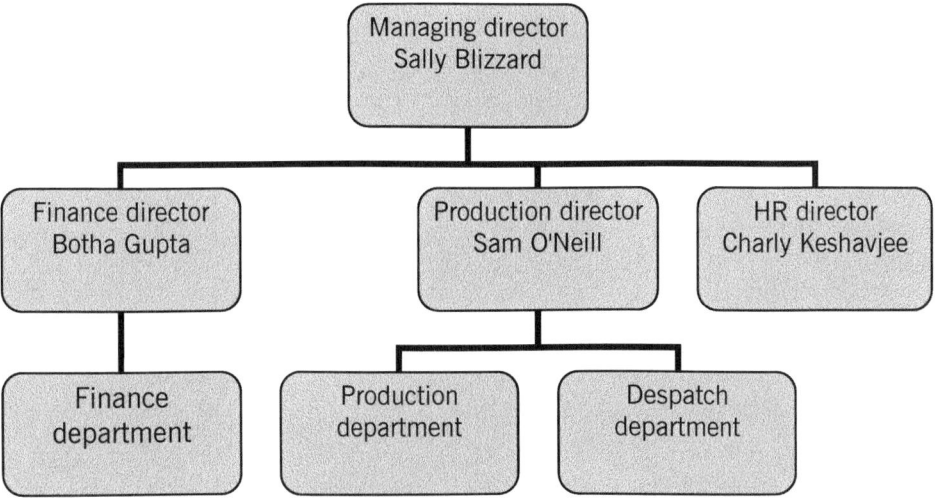

> **KEYWORD**
>
> **Reporting lines** describe the organisational structure determining who is responsible for setting goals and evaluating performance of each staff member.
>
> An **Organisation chart** shows the structure of a business, and the relationships between the different departments.
>
> The **Structure** of an organisation will detail the roles and responsibilities, and often reporting lines and information flow between departments.
>
> **Developing workplace skills** it is important to develop appropriate skills to be effective in the workplace. Some roles have specific technical skill requirements. For instance to work in a finance department you would be likely to need some accounting skills; similarly, to work in the IT department you would need specific IT skills. However, your assessment is concerned with the many workplace skills that are relevant to all those working in an organisation.

2 Developing workplace skills

Nearly all roles that an employee could fill at an organisation involve some degree of interaction with other employees and third parties such as customers and suppliers.

There are a number of workplace practices and behaviours that, if adopted by employees, are likely to lead to greater organisational efficiency. In addition they are likely to lead to an individual being more successful in their job.

Responsibilities of the employee and employer

Organisations are required by law and industry regulations to make sure that they meet certain rules and standards when running their business, for example that the organisation keeps data about its customers secure and confidential.

To ensure that they meet their obligations, organisations set **policies** and **procedures** for employees to follow. These policies and procedures are like a rule book and instruction manual which tell employees how to perform their job and act within the workplace. If all employees follow these rules then the business will be meeting its legal and regulatory obligations.

Policies and procedures can be specific to particular roles (such as rules in a finance team regarding handling petty cash) or apply to all employees (such as health and safety rules).

It is the **responsibility of all employees** to make sure that they comply with any policies and procedures they are given by their employer. If they do not, then the employer may take disciplinary action against them.

As part of health and safety rules, employees have a responsibility to do what they can to keep themselves and others safe while in the workplace and to report any health and safety risks that the find.

It is the **responsibility of the employer** to provide all employees with information regarding all the policies and procedures that they need to know. New employees should be given an induction which covers these policies. Existing employees should be told about any new policies and procedures that affected them and either be given copies of them or be told where to find them.

Under health and safety law, employers have a duty to provide all employees with a safe working environment.

Working with others

Working effectively with others is particularly important when employees work in teams. If a team works more effectively it is more likely to achieve the goals set for it. Working as a team is likely to lead to:

- **Collaboration**: Collaboration is where individuals work together to achieve something. Working as a team means working as a group to fulfil a purpose.

- **Sharing ideas** Members of teams communicate with each other to discuss what needs to be done and the best way to achieve it. Team members will also share ideas to meet the objectives they have, for example to design a new product. By sharing ideas, the overall product is likely to be far superior than what it would be if the team did not exist. Very often ideas will spark new, better ideas.

- **Better team morale**: If goals are achieved or exceeded all members of the team are likely to feel a sense of shared success and be more motivated in future. If the team fails to meet goals its members are likely to be less motivated, may feel a sense of failure and may look to blame individual team members.

- **Achieving goals**: Properly set team goals should be designed to assist in achieving organisational goals. Therefore if individual team goals are met the organisation is more likely to reach its objectives.
- **Utilising individuals' skills and expertise**: Members of a team are individuals with different backgrounds, skills, experience and ideas. Teams can work more effectively than individuals because roles can be given to individuals that already have the skills and experience needed to perform them. Therefore the team can get on with achieving its objectives without the need for members to learn the necessary skills first. Using specialists also means that it is likely that the overall standard of the work will be higher.
- **Shared learning**: Where team members learn new skills or gain knowledge, this information can be shared throughout the team. This increases the knowledge of the whole team quickly, rather than all teams members having to go through the learning process themselves.

How it works

Effective team working involves the following characteristics:

Characteristic	Explanation
Leadership	All teams need a leader, but not all team members can be involved in leadership. Any effective team should have a nominated team leader. Leadership requires a number of skills including organisation, communication and the ability to motivate.
Clear roles and responsibilities	The team leader is responsible for clearly communicating to each team member their role and objectives. If this is not done, work may be duplicated or omitted.
Respect	Members of a team will have different strengths and weaknesses. Each member of the team should be given tasks appropriate to their skills. The way team members interact with each other should be respectful and recognise each person's contribution.
Trust	Team members are dependent on each other in achieving goals. Therefore they need to feel that they can rely on each other. Behaviour such as seeking to blame other team members for problems or not working as hard as other team members can undermine trust.
Co-operation	A team member experiencing problems should be given assistance, not simply criticised. If a team member has finished an assigned task, they should seek to assist a team member falling behind, not take a rest.

Characteristic	Explanation
Common goals	As well as having a clear understanding of their own role, team members need a shared understanding of their common goal.
Realistic deadlines	When a team leader sets goals it is important that these are not unrealistic. Being asked to perform a task that cannot be done in the time allotted will be very demotivating.
Good communication skills	Communication should be two way. The team leader needs to communicate goals. Team members need to provide feedback to the leader and ask for help if additional information or resources are required.
Timekeeping	Members of the team should ensure they arrive for work and meetings on time and keep to break times that are set for them. Being late or taking extended breaks will impact on other team members.
Reliability	Teams work best when everyone can rely on everyone else to do what they said they would do by the time they said they would do it. Work often flows from one team member to another so everyone is relied upon for the team to be able to meet its objectives on time.
Professionalism	Professionalism is about performing your role to the level of skill or experience that you have. Team members need to be open about where they lack knowledge or skills and should go about their business with a focused, business-like manner.

TASK 3 Indicate which of the following is an example of behaviour consistent with effective team working:

(i) Telling a team member who is falling behind that they are useless and letting the team down

(ii) The team leader asking team members to sort out who will perform each task among themselves

(iii) Working extremely hard so that you are able to finish your task and leave work early that day

(iv) Informing the team leader that you have found the task assigned to you difficult and that you are falling behind schedule

Time management

At its simplest, time management means using the available time at work to achieve as much as possible. This involves using time efficiently by prioritising tasks effectively.

As an employee you have limited time to accomplish the objectives set. Therefore it is important to get the most from the scarce resource of time. If employees waste time they are likely to be less successful in achieving their personal goals and in assisting the organisation to meet its objectives.

Meeting deadlines

Poor time management doesn't only adversely affect the individual employee. It can also have implications for:

- The individual's team: A team can be let down by the failure of one of its members to meet a deadline.
- Other employees who depend on the individual's work: For example, a production process may consist of a number of processes performed in sequence. If, due to poor time management, one employee fails to complete the part of the process for which they are responsible on time, other employees later in the production process may also be unable to meet their targets.

How it works

For example, if the sales clerk does not process invoices, the credit controller will not have an up-to-date record of who owes money, and when it's due. As another example, if a purchases clerk does not process invoices, the payments clerk does not know who to pay, or when.

This is another reason why communication is vital: if one person is going to miss a deadline, it may mean that everyone in the team goes on to miss their own deadlines, and the work of the whole function becomes inefficient.

Time management tools

Planning is an important aspect of time management. There are a number of planning aids that can be used to assist in effective time management.

Tool	Description
Diaries	A workplace diary is used to record things that you need to do such as appointments, meetings and task deadlines. Because it is organised by date, it makes it easy to quickly see what commitments you have on a given day. Traditionally diaries were books in which you wrote the details, whereas today it is more likely to be software on your computer or phone.
Online calendars	In the past, a calendar was something you hung on the wall, or kept on a desk which showed the dates of the month whereas a diary was a book. With the move of such tools onto your computer or phone the distinction between diary and calendar has become blurred and the words have become largely interchangeable. For example 'Calendar' in Microsoft Outlook performs the functions of what would have been traditionally described as a diary.
Work schedule	A work schedule also records outstanding tasks. However, it is slightly different to a calendar/diary as it will contain not just task deadlines, but also allocate available time to each task. So a work schedule shows when work is scheduled to be done, not just when it must be done by. This helps to allocate your time to tasks.
To-do lists	A to-do list records outstanding things that you have to do. This might include phone calls, meetings, outstanding tasks etc. A to-do list is a valuable tool for ensuring you don't forget to do something when you are busy. To-do lists may be maintained on paper or on your computer.
Checklists	Checklists are also a tool to avoid forgetting a task. Checklists are a list of standard procedures or tasks that need to be performed. As these tasks are performed they are 'ticked off' to ensure that none are omitted. For example, the end of each month is usually a busy time for an organisation's accounts department and a month-end checklist could be used to make sure nothing is overlooked.
Online collaboration	Online collaboration is where team members use the internet and online tools to work together even though they may be in different physical locations. Tools such as Microsoft Teams and Zoom allow team members to interact, share ideas and work on documents such as spreadsheets at the same time.

Prioritising tasks

All the tools above assist effective time management by recording things that an employee has to do. Knowing what you have to do is an important first stage, but you then need to apply another key skill by **prioritising** these tasks appropriately. In prioritising a task it will be necessary to estimate how long each task is likely to take.

Prioritisation involves a consideration of the **importance** and **urgency** of a task.

Importance relates to whether the performance of other tasks by that employee or others depends on its completion, as well as the person who is to receive the information. The more senior the individual, the more important the task is.

Urgency relates to the task's deadline. Tasks become more urgent the closer you are to the deadline.

> **Exam Focus Point**
>
> Students often struggle with prioritising tasks in the assessment, as stated in a previous Examiner's Report . Students need to ensure they revise the prioritisation of tasks carefully, starting with completing tasks which have a defined deadline then working through any remaining tasks.

TASK 4 Prioritisation

Today is 14 September and you have three tasks on your to-do list.

Task	Description	Completion required by
A	Get filing up to date	15 September
B	Prepare estimates for purchasing department of raw materials required in October	15 September
C	Calculate material usage for the month and provide to accounts	30 September

You enjoy calculating material usage for task C; however you find preparing estimates for Task B more difficult and have been putting it off. Task A, getting your filing up to date, is something you always aim do by the middle of the month and you include it on your to-do list to prevent your filing getting out of control.

What order should you perform these tasks in?   ☐ ☐ ☐

Professional behaviour

As an employee you will be expected to conduct yourself in a professional manner consistent with your role.

As a finance professional you will be expected to comply with confidentiality rules. **Confidentiality** means not sharing information unless you have been authorised or you have a legal or professional duty or right to do so. In particular, you should comply with the **General Data Protection Regulations** and the **Data Protection Act** which control how organisations collect, process and store information about individuals such as customers. You must comply with these rules or there could be legal consequences for you and you organisation.

Following policies and procedures

Some aspects of what is expected of you will be set out in writing by your employer in employment policies or procedures. These could be included in your employment contract, but are more likely to be contained in a procedures manual, employee handbook or similar.

How it works

The following are examples of issues covered by an employer's procedures and policies:

Issue	Explanation
Sustainability	Employees are expected to have an awareness of environmental issues and how their organisation seeks to act sustainably. This may include, for example, reducing wasted energy by turning lights and heat off if not needed and recycling materials where possible.
Use of personal phones	If an employee spends time on a personal phone this reduces their effectiveness and may also disturb others. Therefore a policy may state that personal phone usage should be kept to a minimum.
Use of social media	Use of social media either via a personal phone or an office computer while at work also reduces an employee's effectiveness. Company policy is likely to prohibit use of social media at work. Additionally it may specify that employees should not make social media posts related to their work activities even when using social media out of work as this may breach confidentiality.

Issue	Explanation
Dress code	Many roles will have guidelines regarding what an employee wears. For example, if a role involves dealing face-to-face with customers, employees are likely to be required to be smart and neat in their appearance. Some employees may be required to wear a uniform. Other more detailed policies may cover areas such as jewellery or hairstyle. This could be safety related such as a prohibition on long loose hair or long earrings in a factory environment with machinery.
Answering the phone	Many employees may be responsible for answering business phone calls such as those from customers or suppliers. Some companies have detailed procedures regarding phone interactions to ensure that employees greet customers/suppliers appropriately, provide all necessary information and collect information needed by the business.

Timekeeping

Another important aspect of professional behaviour is good time keeping. An employee who is continually late or fails to make appointments reduces not just their own efficiency, but also that of others.

Good timekeeping encompasses the following:

- Arriving at work on time
- Not leaving early
- Keeping to specified break times
- Arriving promptly to meetings and appointments
- Discussing workloads with a supervisor if you feel you may not meet deadlines

Polite communication

In addition to reducing your own efficiency, arriving late is discourteous to those you have kept waiting.

There are other aspects of politeness that are part of the standards of professional behaviour expected of employees. These include:

Using correct names: Calling a co-worker by a nickname or a contraction of their full name is not appropriate unless it has been made clear that it is how they wish to be addressed.

Avoiding slang and swearing: Co-workers and others you come into contact with may be offended by swearing and slang. Remember just because you would not be offended doesn't mean others aren't.

Avoiding offensive humour: Telling a joke may offend those who are the butt of the joke. It could also have a theme that some find offensive. Humour is a very difficult area to get right in a diverse workplace, as what one individual finds amusing may highly offend another person. Good advice in relation to jokes might be 'if in doubt don't tell it'.

Listening to other people: Virtually all job roles involve meetings and discussions with other people. Remember that these interactions should be two way: listening to others is as important as speaking. Speaking over other people is clearly impolite, but it is also important to make it clear that you are listening to what others say.

Basic courtesy: This is important regardless of how busy you are. Saying 'please' and 'thank you' takes no time and failure to do so may be perceived as a deliberate sleight. The use of polite courtesy is expected in personal interactions, both verbal and in writing.

Personal qualities

Being professional also means demonstrating the following personal qualities.

Honesty: Being honest is not only being truthful, but also being straightforward and transparent in your dealings and relationships, for example not withholding information or hiding it from others.

Adaptability: Being adaptable means being able to respond to change and using your skills and experience in different situations or for different tasks than you may be used to.

Trustworthiness: Having people's trust requires honesty and reliability. People will only trust you if they believe what you say and that you will do what you say you will when you say it will be done by.

Commitment: Being committed means sticking to a task and seeing it through to completion. Not all tasks will go smoothly and being committed requires you to manage and work around problems that you encounter rather than giving up.

TASK 5 Indicate which of the following describes the personal quality of honesty:

(i) Responding to change and using your skills and experience in different situations or for different tasks than you may be used to

(ii) Being straightforward and transparent in your dealings and relationships

(iii) Sticking to a task and seeing it through to completion

(iv) Not sharing information unless you have been authorised or you have a legal or professional duty or right to do so

Workplace communication

Fifty years ago there were only three main forms of communication: face-to-face, telephone or in writing. In the world of today there are now many other forms of electronic communication that may be used in the workplace.

How it works

The following are examples of types of workplace communication:

Communication	Explanation
Face-to-face	Although it may be more time consuming, face-to-face communication can have advantages. Non-verbal communication can reduce the potential for misunderstandings. Something as simple as knowing whether someone is smiling may affect your understanding of how serious a comment is.
Telephone	Although you can't see the person you can still hear 'how' something is said. This still reduces the potential for misunderstanding. However, a phone call is not possible if the person isn't free to take the call. Like face-to-face communication, it requires both parties to be simultaneously available.
Letter	Letters lack the immediacy of direct communication. They are also slow as the letter has to reach the intended recipient before it can be read. However, there is the advantage that a letter is permanent and is useful for setting out complex matters clearly. Also a letter is seen as more formal and might be used for a situation such as making a complaint.
Email	Email has the advantage over a letter of immediate delivery to the recipient (although they still have to open and read it). By convention emails tend to be written in a less formal style than a traditional letter.
Instant messaging	This real-time text-based direct communication method is more immediate than email. This might be used internally in an organisation as a short request for information. It is often used with customers as a way of offering online website help. The style of communication tends to be even less formal than email and is most suited to short messages that require an immediate response.
Reports	These are a standardised way of presenting information. An example might be a monthly sales report that you send to the sales manager. This may well be an electronic rather than a physical document that you attach to an email. Reports are a way of presenting information rather than just a communication method.

Communication	Explanation
Spreadsheets	If you wish to present numerical information this may be done using a spreadsheet. A spreadsheet is just a digital table of numbers. If you send a monthly sales report to the sales manager it may well contain a spreadsheet, perhaps breaking down sales at each branch per week.
Online meetings	Software such as Microsoft Teams and Zoom allow audio and audio/visual meetings to take place. These are a direct replacement for face-to-face meetings when attendees are large distances apart or cannot spare the travel time to meet. Online meetings also allow the sharing of files and other forms of collaboration.
Hybrid working	Many employers now allow employees to split their work time between the office and home. It allows employees to create a better work-life balance as well as bringing other benefits such as cost savings to both the employee and employer.
Intranet	Intranets are a form of internet, but within an organisation. They use a similar browser and allow the organisation to share important information (such as policies and procedures) with employees in a single space.
Shared communication channels	Communication channels are methods of communication (such as online meetings, instant messaging, emails and telephone calls) as well as channels for sharing documents. Effective teams flexibly use different communication methods at the same time, using the most appropriate method to them; for example team members joining in online at a face-to-face meeting. Shared communication also enables teams to work collaboratively on a document. For example, multiple team members can work on updating a budget spreadsheet at the same time.

Within the work environment there are a number of software applications that may be used to assist with communications. These include:

- **Spreadsheet software**: Used to create, view and amend spreadsheets
- **Word processing software**: Used to create documents such as letters and reports. These may be physically printed and sent to a recipient or attached to an email in electronic form.
- **Presentation software**: Allows the user to create slides that make up a presentation. Such presentations may be sent to a recipient to view (electronically or physically), or may be used to support a presentation that an individual delivers.
- **Email software**: Used both for the creation and sending of emails, and to view, store and manage emails that are received.

In your assessment, questions may require you to select the most appropriate method for a given workplace communication. You may also need to know which type of software would be used to support a given workplace communication.

TASK 6 Using an appropriate communication method

Select the most appropriate method of communication in each of the situations in the finance department below.

Notifying a customer who has failed to pay an invoice that you intend to take legal action.

Asking the sales department for the total of last week's sales.

Discussing job performance with an employee.

Options:

Email
Face-to-face
Letter
Report

Information security

In the workplace, information is very often sensitive; the organisation could be harmed if it became public. The organisation needs to keep that information private, in other words secret, within the organisation. Another word for this privacy is **confidentiality**.

> **KEYWORD**
>
> **Confidentiality** is the concept of keeping sensitive information private.

Why might a business want to keep information confidential?

Customers might not be happy at the amount of profit that the organisation makes on sales to them, and buy from someone else...

Suppliers might not be happy at the amount of profit that the organisation makes on items that the suppliers sell to the organisation, so they may raise their prices, or attempt to cut out the organisation and sell direct to its customers...

If sensitive information becomes public knowledge, it can be very damaging to the organisation and even affect whether it can continue trading.

There is even information produced by an organisation that it might not want its own staff to know:

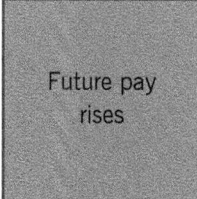
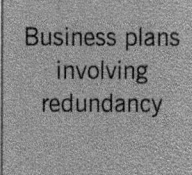

There are many other reasons, beyond simple confidentiality, for organisations to keep information and data secure. These include:

- **Avoiding loss**: The loss of valuable information could cause direct loss to an organisation – for example, if an organisation loses the information about which customers owe it money.
- **Avoiding computer failures and viruses**: A failure to keep data secure could give criminals access to an organisation's computer systems. This could allow the criminal to damage computer systems, for example by computer viruses.
- **Protecting customer information**: Even if loss of data does not affect a company directly, it could adversely affect its customers. This would be the case if customers' credit card details got into the hands of criminals.
- **Legal requirements**: The UK, like most countries, has specific laws placing specific responsibilities on how organisations hold and use personal data.
- **Protects business and personal reputation**: Breaches of confidentiality can damage the reputation of the person whose information was released. The individual who caused the confidentiality breach will also have their reputation damaged as they might not be trusted with confidential information in the future. Depending on the severity of the breach, the business' reputation can be damaged as customers view the business as one which cannot be trusted to keep information secure.

1: Working in the business environment

So, how does an organisation keep information and data secure?

How it works

The ways in which an organisation's data and information are kept secure include the following:

Passwords	Most information in an organisation is usually held in digital form in its IT system. Therefore it is important to control access to this system. If each staff member needs a password to access IT systems it can help to prevent unauthorised persons getting access. Effective passwords should be selected by employees that cannot easily be guessed. So passwords like 'password', 1234, your name or the company name should be avoided. The most effective passwords include letters and numbers as well as special characters such as '#' or '@'. A mixture of upper and lower case letters also makes a password more effective.
Screensavers	Laptops and desktop computers can switch on a screensaver after a particular period of inactivity and require the entry of a password to get back to the user's home screen.
Encryption	Software, such as file compression software and messaging software can encrypt files and messages to ensure only the intended recipient of the information can decipher and read it. This protects the information while it is being communicated.
Firewalls	Software which is designed to prevent unauthorised access to a system by blocking intruders or malicious software at the point of entry into the system.
Secure networks	With remote and hybrid working, employees are transmitting data and accessing corporate information from locations outside of the control of the business. Virtual Private Networks (VPNs) are an example of a secure network that the user can use to access the organisation's information system by entering a password or some other type of authentication.
Back-ups	Regularly copying all data and storing it at another location enables an organisation to restore it in the event it is damaged or lost. For example data can be backed up to the cloud or on hard media which is archived.
	Care must be taken to use appropriate methods to secure back-ups such as restricting access to hard media using physical access restrictions such as locks and keypad entry, and using appropriate cybersecurity methods if backing up to the cloud.

Access restrictions	As well as preventing unauthorised third parties from accessing data, passwords can be used to control what parts of the system each employee has access to. Physical access controls are also important. For example, third parties should not be allowed into areas where confidential information is held such as private offices. Similarly, employees should take sensible steps such as keeping sensitive documents in a locked filing cabinet and not looking at sensitive information on a computer screen where it could be observed.
Anti-virus software	Dedicated software can be installed on computer systems to detect computer viruses that could damage systems and data. Once installed such systems automatically provide protection against viruses.
Authentication to access cloud-based information	To access cloud-based information, such as shared documents, users are required to verify their identity through the use of passwords or codes sent to a mobile device.
Not sharing computers	Each individual should have their own laptop or desktop computer that only they can access files on.
Securing confidential information	Information should only be shared with authorised personnel – those who are permitted to be in contact with it. Information should be protected from non-authorised personnel by not leaving it on desks or in other public areas where it can be seen and by not discussing it in public areas where it may be overheard. Care should be taken when sending emails, for example ensuring that the correct recipient is in the address bar before sending the email.
Cookies and privacy settings	Computers and mobile devices should have their cookie and privacy settings controlled to ensure maximum privacy and security on a corporate device. For example, tracking cookies should be disabled.

TASK 7 Effective passwords

Which of the following would be the most secure password for an employee called Amir Singh?

AmirS ☐

PASSWORD ☐

Computer ☐

@mirS1ngh23 ☐

There are a number of threats to the security of data and information.

How it works

The ways in which an organisation's data and information are kept secure include the following:

Viruses	Malicious software which is designed to damage, destroy, or steal information from an organisation's system. They are often very sophisticated to by-pass cybersecurity methods and are often found in innocent-looking software which users install on their machine.
Hacking	Deliberate attempts by individuals outside of an organisation to gain entry into its system. They often use sophisticated software to guess passwords or find loopholes in security that they can exploit to gain access.
Phishing	Emails or messages that look like they are from a trusted source (such as a bank) which encourage the victim to provide confidential information to the sender so they can gain access to their bank account for example.
System crashes	The hardware that supports a system fails due to issues in the software or physical damage to its components. If a system crashes it will need to be fixed and restarted which may mean data and information are vulnerable for a period of time.

Employee fraud	Employees work from within a system to make a gain for themselves. Data and information is particularly vulnerable if the employee has authorised access to it.
Corrupt files	System crashes and issues when saving files can cause files to turn bad, rendering them impossible to open or use. Regular back-ups is one method of countering this threat, as well as the next two below.
Natural disasters	Fires and floods are examples of natural events that can cause physical damage to a system. They may destroy or damage data held within it.
Accidental deletion	Authorised users accidently delete information while using the system.

3 How sales and purchases support businesses

Not all organisations aim to make a profit, for example charities and some public sector organisations. Those that do are often referred to as businesses. As we have seen, businesses include sole traders, partnerships and companies.

Businesses exist to do something; usually this involves providing goods or services.

Income and expenditure

Businesses receive money from selling goods and services. This is known as income.

Businesses also spend money on goods and services to resell to customers and the costs of running the organisation such as employee wages or electricity. These are known as expenses and expenditure; both terms may be used interchangeably.

The relationship between how much an organisation spends and how much it sells at a given price level determines whether it is successful and whether it is able to continue in business.

Profit and loss

If income exceeds expenses the organisation makes a profit. Alternatively, if expenses exceed income it will make a loss.

If a business is making a profit then it will be generating an overall inflow of money, whereas if it is loss making it will experience an overall outflow of money.

Surplus and deficit

Surplus and deficit are the equivalent terms to profit and loss in a not-for-profit organisation. Surplus occurs where income exceeds expenditure and deficit occurs where expenditure exceeds income.

1: Working in the business environment

> **Exam Focus Point**
>
> The profit of a company is calculated by subtracting the expenses away from income or sales (again, both of these terms may be used interchangeably). If the figure is positive (sales are greater than expenses), then this is a profit. If the figure is negative (the expenses are greater than the sales), then this is a loss. Pay attention to this in your assessment and that you can stipulate whether the business has generated a profit or a loss.

> **KEYWORDS**
>
> **Profit** is what a profit-making organisation makes if income is greater than expenditure in a financial period.
>
> A **loss** is what a profit-making organisation makes if income is less than expenditure in a financial period.
>
> **Surplus** is what a not-for-profit organisation makes if income is greater than expenditure in a financial period.
>
> A **deficit** is what a not-for-profit organisation makes if income is less than expenditure in a financial period.

How it works

Organisation A	£
Income	100,000
Expenditure	80,000
Profit	20,000

Organisation B	£
Income	50,000
Expenditure	75,000
Loss	(25,000)

In these examples:

Organisation A has **spent** £20,000 **less than** it **earned** in the financial period. This is therefore a **profit** for that period.

Organisation B has **spent** £25,000 **more than** it **earned** in the financial period. This is therefore a **loss** for that period.

Note that expenditure is sometimes shown in brackets to show that it is being subtracted from income.

A loss is often shown in brackets to show that it is a negative number, rather than being shown as –£25,000.

The following illustration looks at expenses in more detail. It is important that you read the question carefully.

How it works

You may be required to take away (subtract) one number from another; for example, income minus the expenses related to those sales (cost of sales) is gross profit. To determine net profit, you would then have to subtract a further number (total other expenditure).

	£
Income	100,000
Wages and salaries	20,000
Other expenditure	15,000

Profit = Income – Total expenditure

Profit = Income – Wages and salaries – Other expenditure:

100,000 – 20,000 – 15,000 = 65,000

To do this sum on your calculator, you should:

1 Enter the first figure, which is 100,000
2 Press the – button
3 Enter the second figure, which is 20,000
4 Press the – button
5 (The screen may currently show the gross profit figure)
6 Enter the third figure, which is 15,000
7 Press the = button (this will give the net profit figure)

In the assessment, tasks will often just ask you to 'calculate', so you must decide if addition or subtraction is required. Often a task will require both functions to be performed, such as when completing missing records (see the 'How it works' example below). Take care when assessing whether to subtract (expense) or whether to add (income).

How it works

In the first example below you need to add all the figures to come to the total for parts expenditure at the bottom, which is £182,000. This is adding the column of figures, as seen above.

List of parts	£
Part A	25,000
Part B	54,000
Part C	36,000
Part D	67,000
Total (all parts)	

In the next example, you need to subtract the three given wages and salaries figures from the total figure given, to arrive at the missing administration salaries cost, which is £65,000. The easiest way is to do this in two steps, as shown in the working below the table.

List of wages/salaries costs	£
Factory 1 wages	120,000
Factory 2 wages	140,000
Administration salaries	
Directors' salaries	125,000
Total	450,000

Working:

Step one – add the three wages and salaries costs you have been given.

	£
Factory 1 wages	120,000
Factory 2 wages	140,000
Directors' salaries	125,000
Total of costs itemised	385,000

Step two – subtract this figure from the total given in the original table.

	£
Total cost	450,000
Total of costs itemised	(385,000)
Administration salaries	65,000

Consequences of making losses

If expenditure exceeds sales, a business will make a loss. This leads to an outflow of money from the business and this will not be able to be sustained indefinitely.

Businesses need a supply of money in order to operate, or they may experience the following problems:

- An inability to pay for purchases and meet other expenses such as wages.
- The business' bank account will be reduced and may go into overdraft.
- If suppliers are not paid on time, they may withdraw credit from the business.
- In the long run the business will find it difficult to carry on operating and could fail.

Opportunities from making a profit

If a business' sales exceed expenditure, it will make a profit and will receive an overall inflow of money. This inflow of money can be used in a number of ways to benefit the business or its owners including:

- Further investment in the business to create growth
- Saving or investment in the bank to earn interest
- Repayment of business loans to save interest charges
- Distribution to the business' owners

KEYWORDS

Expenses are the money a business pays out when it spends money to purchase goods or services for the organisation or to resell or to run the organisation.

Income is the money a business receives when it makes sales of goods or services to other parties.

How it works

The following are examples of expenses and income.

Item	Classification	Further definition
Sales of goods	Income	Earnings resulting from selling items to customers
Providing services	Income	Customers pay for receiving a service
Bank interest received	Income	Earnings resulting from having money saved in the bank
Purchases (raw materials or goods for resale)	Expenses	Expenditure on items to produce or sell to customers
Payments to staff	Expenses	Wages and salaries paid to staff working in the business

Item	Classification	Further definition
Insurance	Expenses	Payments to insure assets against loss or damage
Advertising	Expenses	Payments made to advertise an organisation's products
Road tax/fuel/motor expenses	Expenses	Payments made to use an organisation's vehicles

Note. about expenditure: there could be a large number of examples of different services an organisation spends money on. Only a small number have been given here to illustrate – try to think of some more in an organisation with which you are familiar.

TASK 8 Place the items listed below into the appropriate box.

advertising costs, sale, insurance, fuel costs, interest received, interest on a bank overdraft, wages and salaries

Expenses

Income

Sales and purchases

Nearly all businesses seeking to make a profit will make sales and purchases. You need to learn the terminology related to sales and purchases, know typical payments terms and understand their effect on a business' bank account.

Sales

Businesses sell goods to other businesses and individuals. These parties are generally referred to as customers.

A client is someone who engages a professional to provide a service. Someone who uses the services of a lawyer, an accountant or a plumber would typically be referred to as a client rather than as a customer.

However, it should be noted that in practice the terms client and customer can be applied rather loosely and are often used interchangeably.

Cash and credit sales

A customer of a retail shop generally pays for the goods purchased immediately. This is an example of a cash sale.

Alternatively, an organisation may not receive payment for goods or services it sells straightaway because it has extended **credit** to the customer or client. For example many mobile phone subscribers pay their account monthly after the service has been provided. This is because the mobile phone operator has extended credit to them.

Where credit sales are made, the terms of the sale will specify the period of time within which the customer or client has to make payment. We will consider this more when we look at payment terms below.

KEYWORDS

A **customer** is a person or business who buys goods or services.

A **client** is a person who engages the services of a professional.

A **cash sale** is a transaction to sell goods or services for which payment is made immediately.

A **credit sale** is a transaction to sell goods or services when payment is made at a later date than the delivery of goods or provision of the service.

Purchases

A business will also purchase goods and services. The individual from whom a business buys goods and services is known as a supplier. For example, nearly all businesses will use electricity and therefore will have an electricity company as one of their suppliers.

Just as we saw with sales, purchases may be made on a cash basis requiring immediate payment or on a credit basis where payment is made at a later date than the delivery of goods or services.

If a business needs to purchase goods or a service there will often be a large number of potential suppliers. In order to simplify the purchasing process a business may have a list of approved suppliers. These will be suppliers where the business has verified their ability to supply appropriate goods or services at an acceptable price. For example, if a business has a water leak and needs the services of a plumber, rather than having to set about finding a plumber and establishing whether they are reliable and can provide good service at a reasonable price it will be much more efficient to call a plumber from a list of approved suppliers.

KEYWORDS

A **supplier** is a person who sells goods and services to a customer.

A **cash purchase** is a transaction to purchase goods or services for which payment is made immediately.

A **credit purchase** is a transaction to purchase goods or services when payment is made at a later date than the delivery of goods or provision of the service.

Approved suppliers are suppliers where the business has verified their ability to supply appropriate goods or services at an acceptable price.

Exam Focus Point

Ensure that you can explain the differences between sales (and purchases) made in cash and those that are made on credit. Some students are not fully understanding the differences between these transactions in their assessment.

Payment terms

Where goods and services are purchased and sold, the payment terms for the transaction will be agreed by the business and the other party.

The purpose of establishing payment terms for a transaction is to ensure that the customer or client knows when to pay invoices by and to ensure that suppliers are paid at an agreed time.

There are many different payment terms that might be encountered in practice. You should be aware of the following ones:

Payment terms	Meaning
In advance	Payment is required before goods are delivered or services supplied.
On delivery	Sometimes referred to as cash on delivery (or just COD). Generally used in relation to supply of goods where the customer makes payment only when the goods are delivered.

Payment terms	Meaning
Specified period after invoice date	For credit sales the terms of the transaction may specify how long the customer has to make payment after the date of the invoice. Commonly used periods include 10, 14, 30 or 60 days after the invoice date.
Payment by end of month of invoice	All invoices dated in a particular month must be paid by that month end. For example if two invoices are received, one dated 2 May and the other 24 May, both require payment by 31 May. In this situation the period of credit extended to the customer varies depending on the date of the invoice.

How it works

Paper Products is an organisation which makes printed boxes and other items. It has a customer, Applebys, and a supplier, Pearmans. It has **credit** transactions with both of them.

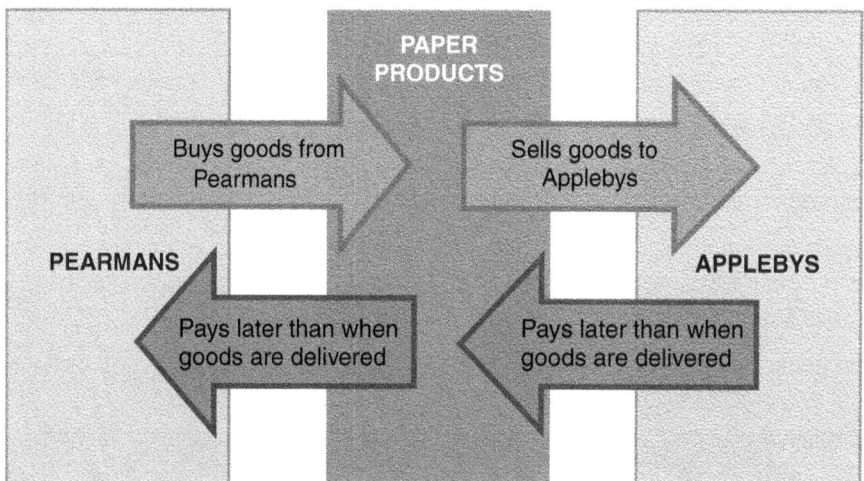

Wood Works is an organisation which makes wooden items. It has a customer, Cherryton, and a supplier, Banarama. It has **cash** transactions with both of them.

1: Working in the business environment

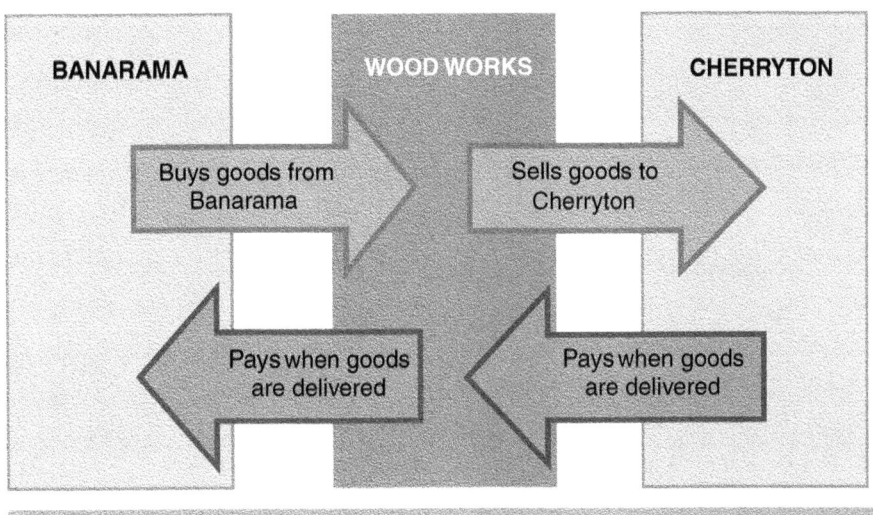

Effect of payment terms on the bank balance

Payment terms affect when a business receives payment for sales and makes payment for purchases. Because of this the payment terms of a business' transactions have an effect on its bank balance.

For example, if on the same day a business makes a purchase of goods for £100 and sells them on to a customer for £120 the business has made a profit of £20. You might expect that this would lead to the business' bank balance increasing by the £20 of profit. This would be the case if both sale and purchase were for cash. However, assume that the payment terms for the purchase were cash on delivery and for the sale 30 days after invoice date. In this situation the business pays out £100 immediately and may only receive the £120 from the sale 30 days after the invoice date. Therefore the business' bank balance would fall by £100 until payment is received for the sale, which could take 30 days.

TASK 9 **Place the items listed below into the appropriate box.**

Sale of goods when payment is made at a date later than delivery

Sale of goods when cash is paid on delivery

Sale of services when cash is paid at a date later than the service was provided

Sale of services when cash is paid on delivery of the service

Purchase of goods when payment is made at the same time as delivery of the goods

Purchase of services when payment is made at the same time as the service is provided

Purchase of goods when payment is made at a date later than delivery

Purchase of a service when payment is made at a later date than the service is provided

Cash sale	Credit sale
Cash purchase	Credit purchase

TASK 10 (a) The balance of an organisation's income and expenditure results in profit or loss.

Which ONE of the following statements is true?

When income exceeds profit, an organisation has made a loss. ☐

When income exceeds expenditure, an organisation has made a profit. ☐

When income exceeds expenditure, an organisation has made a loss. ☐

(b) The balance of an organisation's income and expenditure results in profit or loss.

Which ONE of the following statements is true?

When expenditure exceeds profit, an organisation has made a loss. ☐

When expenditure exceeds income, an organisation has made a profit. ☐

When expenditure exceeds income, an organisation has made a loss. ☐

(c) Which one of the following would increase a business' bank balance?

Reducing the period of time before customers have to pay ☐

Agreeing to pay suppliers in cash, rather than on credit ☐

Introducing increased credit terms for customers. ☐

(d) Which one of the following would NOT be a likely consequence of a business making losses?

Insufficient money to make purchases ☐

The ability to increase investment in the business ☐

An overdraft on the business' bank account ☐

(e) Using the information in the first two tables, place a tick in the appropriate column of the third table below to show whether each of the organisations has made a profit or a loss. You should not place more than one tick (✓) against each organisation.

Organisation A	
	£
Income	80,000
Expenditure	70,000

Organisation B	
	£
Income	150,000
Expenditure	120,000

Organisation	Profit	Loss
Organisation A		
Organisation B		

4 Sales and purchase procedures

Organisations have standardised procedures related to both sales and purchases. These procedures aim to standardise the way in which purchases and sales are done, regardless of the staff members involved.

As part of its business procedures for sales and purchases a business will use a number of different types of documents.

Business procedures and documents

The objectives of standardised business procedures and documents are:

- **The prevention of errors**: Procedures help to ensure that all relevant information is provided and can incorporate authorisation checks.

- **The promotion of efficiency**: Using consistent procedures and filling out standard documentation is easier than starting from scratch. Greater efficiency reduces the likelihood of missing deadlines.

- **To ensure that all necessary information is collected**: A business will require certain information for accounting and tax purposes. Documentation can be designed to ensure that this information is captured so that business processes can be completed as required.

- **To avoid disputes with customers and suppliers:** Preparing standard documents containing all the relevant information related to a transaction reduces the chance of a disagreement with a customer or supplier and helps to promote good customer/supplier relations.

Any system is only effective if it is adhered to. Therefore, it is important that all members of an organisation's staff follow procedures carefully. This includes filling out any documents accurately and in full. It may be tempting to 'cut corners' and not complete documents properly. This might involve:

- Not completing documents in full
- Not obtaining required authorisations
- Not completing documents on time

However, you should avoid such practices as this can lead to problems such as errors, disputes and incorrect information and in the long run reduce business efficiency.

Business procedures for sales

For credit sales the process starts with an order from a customer. The **customer order** could be received from the customer by mail or email or the order could be received by phone and recorded on a standardised form. This form will record the details of the goods or services that the customer wishes to buy.

If the transaction relates to the supply of goods, when the goods are sent to the customer they will be accompanied by a **delivery note** which contains details of what has been supplied and describes the order to which they relate.

A **sales invoice** will then be generated describing the goods supplied, the order it relates to and the amount due and specifying the payment terms. When the invoice is raised, the income will be recorded by the business. Although the cash has not yet been received, this sale is still recorded with an outstanding payment from the customer (referred to as a debtor or receivable).

We will look at exactly what information these documents should contain in a moment.

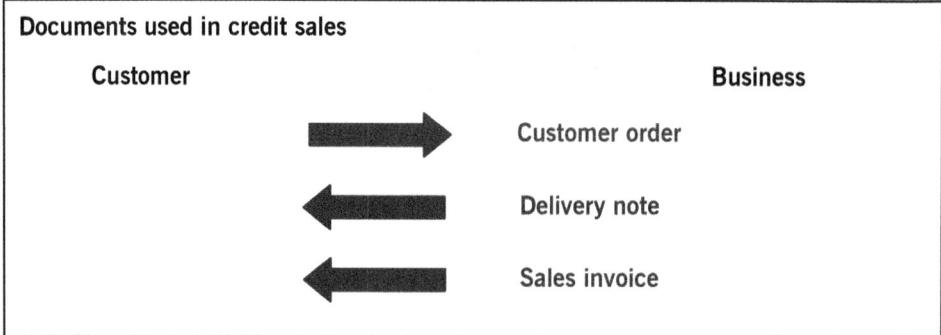

Business procedures for purchases

Firstly, a supplier must be selected. Most organisations will maintain an **approved supplier list** from which a supplier must be selected. If there is not an approved supplier for the goods or services required there is typically an authorisation process to ensure the supplier is appropriate.

Next, the organisation raises a **purchase order** which it sends to the selected supplier.

The organisation will then receive the goods or services requested. The organisation will receive a **delivery note** from the supplier along with the goods. The supplier typically requires someone at the business to sign a copy of the delivery note to acknowledge that the goods were received in good condition.

Goods are likely to be received into a warehouse or goods inwards department. This department will check and record what has been delivered, compare it to the delivery note and record any discrepancy. An internal document recording goods received will be raised (known as a **goods received note**, GRN) and is evidence that the goods ordered were received. A comparison of a GRN to the purchase order will reveal any discrepancies in what was delivered compared to what was ordered. Any such discrepancies will need to be queried with the supplier.

After the goods have been delivered the supplier will send the **purchase invoice**. A business will check the GRN/delivery note against the purchase invoice and the purchase order before making payment. Otherwise there is a risk that payment will be made for goods that haven't been received or were not ordered in the first place.

Having satisfied itself that the invoice related to goods both ordered and delivered payment will be made.

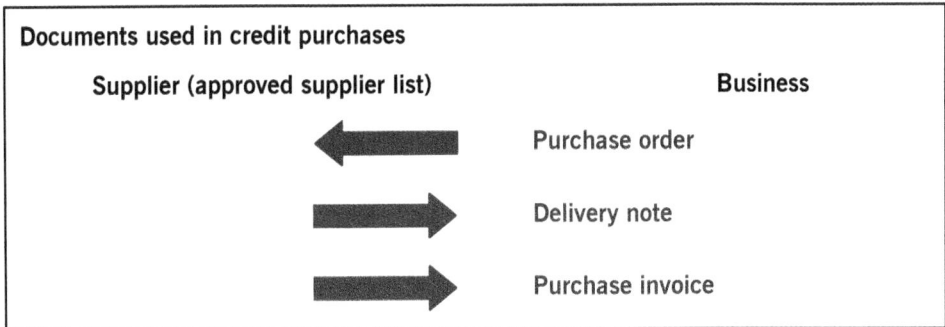

TASK 11 Identify which one of the statements below is correct.

A goods received note is produced by a supplier.	☐
A delivery note should state the purchase order number.	☐
A purchase invoice should state the customer order number.	☐
A customer invoice should always require payment before goods are delivered.	☐

KEYWORDS

A **purchase invoice** is the document a supplier gives an organisation in relation to a purchase of goods on credit. It indicates the amount owed and when that amount is due for payment.

A **sales invoice** is the document a business gives a customer in relation to a sale of goods on credit. It indicates the amount owed and when that amount is due for payment.

A **purchase order** is the document a business provides to a supplier requesting that the supplier sells the organisation the goods stated on the order.

A **customer order** is the document a business receives from a customer requesting that the organisation sells the goods stated on the order.

A **delivery note** is the document accompanying goods when they are delivered. It describes the goods being delivered and the order and invoice they relate to.

A **goods received note (GRN)** when the goods ordered by a business are received the GRN is prepared recording the details of what was received. This is an internal document and should be compared to the invoice before payment.

Note. An organisation is both a customer and a supplier – so, for example, it will both receive and send both orders and invoices.

How it works

Here are examples of the documents described above:

SALES INVOICE	Invoice number 56314
Haywood Distributors Industrial Estate Haywood HY4 2SK Tel: 01234 563939	
VAT registration:	0274 2694 49
Date/tax point:	7 September 20XX
Order number:	32011
Customer:	Freeway Superstores 28 Liberty Park Haywood HY4 5TR
Account number (customer code)	HD 35

Description/product code	Quantity	Unit amount £	Total £
Sondy Flat Screen TVs /3200IST25	6	300.00	1,800.00
Net total			1,800.00
VAT at 20%			360.00
Invoice total			2,160.00
Terms 30 days net			

- Supplier
- Invoice date
- Customer
- Items being sold
- Tax
- Period after which payment is due

ORDER

FREEWAY SUPERSTORES
28 Liberty Park
Haywood HY4 5TR
Tel 0303446 Fax 0303447

(Customer)

To: Haywood Distributors
Industrial Estate
Haywood
HY4 2SK

Number: 32011

Date: 5 Sept 20XX

Delivery address: Freeway Superstores
28 Liberty Park
Haywood HY4 5TR

Product code	Quantity	Description	Unit list price £
4425	6	Sondy Flat Screen TVs	300 (excluding VAT)

(Items to be bought)

Authorised by: P. Winterbottom   **Date:** 5 Sept 20XX

DELIVERY NOTE   Number: HAY0345

Deliver to: Freeway Superstores 28 Liberty Park Haywood HY4 5TR	Supplier: Haywood Distributors Industrial Estate Haywood HY4 2SK Tel: 01234 563939					
Date: 6 September 20XX						
Account number (customer code)			HD 35			
Order number	Description	Unit price	Quantity	Total Price (net)	VAT	Total Price (Gross)
32011	Sondy Flat Screen TV	300	6	1800	360	2160
Total			6	1800	360	2160
	Received in good condition.					
Name:			Signature:			

- Customer
- Supplier
- List items delivered
- Discrepancies or damage noted
- Signed by staff member to acknowledge receipt

GOODS RECEIVED NOTE

Supplier →

Delivery from: Haywood Distributors Industrial Estate Haywood HY4 2SK	GRN Number:	00394
	Supplier code:	02-756

Date received:	6 September 20XX
Account number (customer code)	HD 35

List items received →

Order number	Description	Unit price	Quantity	Total Price (net)	VAT	Total Price (Gross)
32011	Sondy Flat Screen TV	300	6	1800	360	2160
Total			6	1800	360	2160

Received by:

....

← Signed by staff member

You need to know the purpose of each of the document types above, the information they contain and be able to identify errors and discrepancies.

TASK 12 The invoice below has been received from a supplier.

INVOICE	Invoice number 2389
EZ Stationary Supplies Church Lane Woodfield WF4 8GT Tel: 02143 555009	
VAT registration:	0345 7688 21
Date/tax point:	12 June 20XX
Customer number	1204
Customer:	General Builders Ltd 13E South Street Woodfield WF7 9HJ
Account number (customer code)	GB/134

Description/product code	Quantity	Unit amount £	Total £
A4 Photocopy paper – Ream	50	3.50	192.50
Net total			192.50
VAT at 20%			38.50
Invoice total			231.00
Payment terms – End of invoice month			

(a) **What information is missing from this invoice?**

    The purchase order number ☐
    The GRN number ☐
    The order date ☐

(b) **Once you have obtained the purchase order number which of the following is the appropriate action in respect of this invoice?**

    The amount of £231 should be paid by the end of June. ☐
    The invoice amount should be queried with the supplier. ☐
    The amount of £192.50 should be paid by the end of June. ☐

    You need to know the purpose of each of the document types above, the information they contain and be able to identify errors and discrepancies.

Chapter overview

There are many organisations that exist to make a profit, but there are also organisations with different aims such as the public sector and charities.

Businesses fall into different sectors such as services, retail and manufacturing.

All but the smallest organisations are organised into departments with specific responsibilities.

Organisations have reporting lines which determine who sets each employee's goals and evaluates their performance.

Effective employees need to develop a number of workplace skills.

Nearly all jobs involve some degree of working with others, which makes teamwork important.

Time is a scarce resource and it is important to adopt practices that lead to good time management.

All employees are expected to adhere to professional standards of behaviour such as having good timekeeping and communicating in a polite manner.

There are a number of procedures that an organisation can use to keep information and data secure, including passwords and physical access controls.

Communication skills are very important in the workplace. Part of this is knowing which communication methods are appropriate to a given situation.

Computer data and other information held by organisations may be sensitive and should be kept confidential.

Information and data is a valuable asset for organisations so its loss or destruction may be costly. There are many steps that can be taken to avoid this, such as installing anti-virus software on IT systems and using effective passwords.

Organisations usually exist to do something. Many organisations buy and sell things.

You must learn the definitions of expenditure and income, profit and loss and understand them well enough to do simple calculations.

Businesses make both sales and purchases. You need to know terminology related to sales and purchases as well as typical payments terms and understand their effect on a business' bank account.

Organisations make both cash and credit transactions. A credit transaction is when payment is delayed over a prearranged period.

Businesses have standard business processes in relation to sales and purchases and these will involve a number of standard document types.

The key documents in relation to sales are:

- Customer order
- Delivery note
- Sales invoice

The key documents in relation to purchases are:

- Purchase order
- Delivery note
- Goods received note
- Purchase invoice

You need to know the purpose of each, information they include and be able to identify errors and discrepancies.

Keywords

APPROVED SUPPLIERS are suppliers where the business has verified their ability to supply appropriate goods or services at an acceptable price.

A **CASH PURCHASE** is a transaction to purchase goods or services when payment is made immediately.

A **CASH SALE** is a transaction to sell goods or services when payment is made immediately.

CHARITIES raise money in order to spend it on a specified purpose.

A **CLIENT** is a person who engages the services of a professional.

COMMERICAL organisations aim to make a profit, usually by selling goods or providing services and are often referred to as businesses.

COMMUNITY AND VOLUNTARY ORGANISATIONS raise money to perform a service in their local area.

COMMUNITY INTEREST COMPANIES (CICs) are a special form of company for use by 'social' enterprises pursuing purposes that are beneficial to the community.

CONFIDENTIALITY is the concept of keeping sensitive information private.

A **CREDIT PURCHASE** is a transaction to purchase goods or services when payment is made at a later date than the delivery of goods or provision of the service.

A **CREDIT SALE** is a transaction to sell goods or services when payment is made at a later date than the delivery of goods or provision of the service.

A **CUSTOMER** is a person who buys goods or services.

A **CUSTOMER ORDER** is the document a business receives from a customer requesting that the organisation sells the goods stated on the order.

A **DEFICIT** is what a not-for-profit organisation makes if income is less than expenditure in a financial period.

A **DELIVERY NOTE** is the document accompanying goods when they are delivered. It describes the goods being delivered and the order and invoice they relate to.

DIVERSITY AND EQUAL OPPORTUNITIES means that organisations should employ people with as wide a range of backgrounds as possible and treat them the same.

ETHICS are a moral guide to behaviour.

EXPENSES are the money a business pays out when it spends money to purchase goods or services for the organisation or to resell or to run the organisation.

A **GOODS RECEIVED NOTE (GRN).** When the goods ordered by a business are received, the GRN is prepared recording the details of what was received. This is an internal document and should be compared to the invoice before payment.

INCOME is the money a business earns when it makes sales of goods or services to other parties.

A **LIMITED COMPANY** is owned by shareholders and run by directors. Some companies are very large.

A **LOSS** is what an organisation makes if income is less than expenditure in a financial period.

An **ORGANISATION CHART** shows the structure of a business, and the relationships between the different departments.

A **PARTNERSHIP** is a business owned and run by a number of individuals.

A **PRIVATE LIMITED COMPANY (LTD)** is a form of limited company that cannot sell its shares to the general public.

PROFIT is what an organisation makes if income is greater than expenditure in a financial period.

A **PUBLIC LIMITED COMPANY (PLC)** is a form of limited company that can sell its shares to the public, for example through a stock market.

Organisations in the **PUBLIC SECTOR** are funded by government to deliver services or achieve government aims.

A **PURCHASE INVOICE** is the document a supplier gives an organisation in relation to a purchase of goods on credit. It indicates the amount owed and when that amount is due for payment.

A **PURCHASE ORDER** is the document a business provides to a supplier requesting that the supplier sells the organisation the goods stated on the order.

A **SALES INVOICE** is the document a business gives a customer in relation to a sale of goods on credit. It indicates the amount owed and when that amount is due for payment.

SOCIAL ENTERPRISES are run like profit-making organisations but invest or donate the money raised to create positive social and environmental change.

A **SOLE TRADER** is a small business run and owned by an individual.

The **STRUCTURE** of an organisation will detail the roles and responsibilities, and often reporting lines and information flow between departments.

A **SUPPLIER** is a person who sells goods and services to a customer.

SURPLUS is what a not-for-profit organisation makes if income is greater than expenditure in a financial period.

SUSTAINABILITY concerns meeting our own needs for today, but not at the expense of future generations.

2 Working in the business environment: Test your learning

This chapter gives you question practice on the topics you covered in the previous chapter. The questions are in the same style you can expect in your assessment. You can find the answers at the back of this Workbook.

1   There are different types of organisation.

   Complete the following sentences by selecting the most appropriate option from the list of items below each sentence.

   (a)   A sole trader is a ⬚ organisation.

   - private sector
   - public sector
   - charitable

   (b)   The police service ⬚ aim to make a profit.

   - does
   - does not

2   It is important to understand the role of the finance department within an organisation.

   Indicate whether the following statements are true or false.

   (a)   Detailed expenditure analysis provided by the finance department of a partnership is used by the general public to make business decisions.

   True   ☐

   False ☐

(b) An organisation's IT department provides a service to customers and suppliers.

True ☐

False ☐

3 It is important to observe confidentiality.

Complete the following sentences by inserting the most appropriate option from the list below each sentence.

Information about pay increases held on a computer should be kept

[   ]

- in an area to which all employees have access.
- in a password-protected file with access restricted to those who need the information.

A supplier of the organisation where you work asks you who the main customers of the organisation are. You reply:

[   ]

- 'I am sorry but I cannot give you any information, as it is confidential.'
- 'As you are a supplier I can tell you that they are Matlins and Swindells.'

4 Employees should behave in a professional manner.

Indicate whether the following statements are true or false.

Frequently arriving late for work is fine if it is because your train is late.

True ☐

False ☐

Use of personal phones at work is acceptable provided that you leave the office to avoid disturbing colleagues.

True ☐

False ☐

5   Methods of workplace communication

    (a) **Complete this sentence by inserting the most appropriate option from the list below each box.**

    Communicating by letter is ☐ for communications when ☐ is not of the highest importance.

    - necessary
    - appropriate
    - inappropriate
    - speed
    - formality
    - privacy

    Working with others

    (b) **Indicate whether the following statements are true or false.**

    Teams work best when members are given clear goals by the team leader.

    True   ☐

    False ☐

    Giving team members unrealistic deadlines will ensure that they work harder.

    True   ☐

    False ☐

6   Time management

    (a) **Complete this sentence by inserting the most appropriate option from the list below each box.**

    Tasks should be allocated to the time available based on their ☐ and their ☐.

    - length
    - urgency
    - importance
    - difficulty

    (b) **Indicate whether the following statements are true or false.**

    Diaries and calendars can be physical documents or computer software.

    True   ☐

    False ☐

    A calendar is the most appropriate tool for making sure that you do not forget to complete a task when you are busy.

    True   ☐

    False ☐

7 Responsibilities of the employer and employee

(a) **Indicate whether the following statement is true or false.**

Employees have a responsibility to report any health and safety risks in the workplace.

True ☐

False ☐

(b) **Indicate whether the following statement is true or false.**

Employers have a responsibility to provide new staff with an induction that covers the organisation's policies and procedures.

True ☐

False ☐

8 Methods of communication

Indicate whether the following statements are true or false.

Hybrid working is where employees decide how many hours they need to work each day.

True ☐

False ☐

Working collaboratively on a document store in the cloud is an example of shared communication channels.

True ☐

False ☐

9 Keeping data and information secure.

Complete the following sentences by inserting the most appropriate option from the list below each sentence.

(a) Locks on filing cabinets where paper copies of confidential documents are kept is an example of

☐

- a secure network
- physical access restrictions.

(b) Software designed to prevent unauthorised access to a system by blocking intruders or malicious software at the point of entry into the system is

[   ]

- encryption
- a firewall

Indicate whether the following statements are true or false.

(c) Encouraging victims to part with confidential information by sending emails from apparently trusted sources is known as hacking.

True ☐

False ☐

(d) Using sophisticated software to guess passwords or find loopholes in security that they can exploit to gain access is known as phishing.

True ☐

False ☐

10 Last year your organisation recorded income and expenditure as shown in the table below.

Income and expenditure	£
Cash sales	380,000
Credit sales	197,500
Wages and salaries	285,900
Other expenses	197,583

(a) Use the income and expenditure figures to complete the following calculations.

(i) **Calculate total expenses:**

£ [   ]

(ii) **Calculate profit:**

£ [   ]

(b) **Using your answer from (a)(ii), calculate profit as a percentage of sales. If your answer is not a whole number, provide your answer to two decimal places.**

[   ] %

11 Organisations have income and expenses.

(a) **Select the appropriate word from the list of terms below to match the description.**

Description	Term described
Money spent by the organisation	
Money earned by the organisation	

List of terms

Income
Expenses

(b) **Select the appropriate word from the list of terms below to match the description.**

Description	Term described
An amount paid to purchase motor insurance	
A sale to a customer on credit	

List of terms

Expense
Income

12 Organisations can make sales and purchases for cash or for credit.

Complete the following sentences by selecting the most appropriate option from the list of terms below.

When an organisation sells goods to a customer and the customer pays for the goods three weeks after the goods are delivered, this is known as a ☐.

When an organisation buys services from a person and pays that person on the day the service is carried out, this is known as a ☐.

List of terms

credit sale
cash sale
credit purchase
cash purchase

13 Organisations issue and receive different documents as part of the business procedures related to buying and selling goods.

Complete the following sentences by selecting the most appropriate option from the list of terms below.

An organisation sends [ ] to a customer for goods sold on credit.

An organisation gets [ ] from a supplier accompanying goods it receives.

An organisation receives [ ] from a customer requesting that goods specified are sold to the customer.

List of terms

an invoice
a purchase order
a delivery note
a customer order
a goods received note

14 An electronics retail business sells three laptop computers to a customer on 23 August on credit and the following invoice has been prepared.

INVOICE	Invoice number 56314
Select Computers Ltd Newtown Industrial Park Newtown NT14 7GG Tel: 0786 55449867	
VAT registration:	0274 2694 49
Date/tax point:	7 September 20XX
Customer:	Bilal's Office Services 2 Church Road Newtown NT3 7DH
Account number (customer code)	HD 35

Description/product code		Total £
Acme S34 Laptops		1,800.00
Net total		1,800.00
VAT at 20%		360.00
Invoice total		2,160.00
Payment terms 21 days		

(a) **Identify TWO items missing from the invoice prepared by Select Computers Ltd from the list below.**

Purchase order number ☐

Quantity supplied ☐

Customer order number ☐

Date goods received ☐

Date goods despatched ☐

Condition of goods received ☐

(b) **Before payment which of the following documents should Bilal's Office Services compare the invoice to?**

Customer order and goods received note ☐

Purchase order and supplier invoice ☐

Customer invoice and delivery note ☐

Purchase order and goods received note ☐

15 A business sends an invoice in respect of goods supplied to a customer on 1 September.

(a) **Which of the following payment terms would lead to the longest period of credit being extended to the customer?**

End of the month of invoice ☐

30 days after invoice date ☐

10 business days after invoice date ☐

(b) **Which of the following actions would NOT be expected to increase a business' bank balance?**

Increasing the period of credit offered to customers ☐

Increasing the amount of sales ☐

Reducing the amount of purchases ☐

Increasing the amount of time taken to pay suppliers ☐

16 A business receives more goods from a supplier than it ordered.

Indicate whether the following statement is true or false.

This discrepancy should be identified by comparing the goods received note to the purchase order.

True ☐

False ☐

17 In February 20XX General Retail Ltd has expenses of £34,509 and makes cash sales of £13,239 and credit sales of £23,446.

(a) **What is the correct figure for the profit or loss for General Retail in February?**

£ ☐

(b) All General Retail's expenses in February are paid by the end of that month. Payment terms offered by General Retail to its customers buying on credit are 60 days after invoice date.

Which of the following is true in relation to the impact of February's trading on General Retail's bank account?

It will cause it to rise. ☐

It will cause it to fall. ☐

It could cause it to fall or rise. ☐

(c) **Which ONE of the following statements is TRUE in relation to General Retail's sales?**

Deliveries of goods to credit customers are always accompanied by a sales invoice. ☐

Payments from credit customers should be checked to goods received notes. ☐

Goods should only be despatched after payment from credit customers has been received. ☐

Customers will raise a query with General Retail if the quantity of goods recorded on a GRN doesn't match the amount ordered. ☐

3 Using numbers in business

Chapter coverage

This chapter covers basic numeracy skills essential for the business environment. This includes recording, sorting and performing common calculations. Candidates need to be able to work with currency, units of time, decimals, fractions and ratios. This chapter assumes that you will take a calculator to your assessment, which you are expected to do.

	Section number
Numbers in business	1
Using a calculator	2
Addition and subtraction	3
Multiplication and division	4
Calculations with time	5
Ratios	6
Proportions as fractions	7
Percentages	8
Fractions	9
Converting percentages, fractions and decimals	10
Averages	11
Presenting numerical data	12

1 Numbers in business

Numbers are a key part of business and are commonly encountered as a monetary amount as well as being used to describe other business characteristics such as the quantity of goods sold.

Numbers can be recorded in figures or words. For example an organisation's current bank balance could be described as £3,451.34 or three thousand, four hundred and fifty one pounds and thirty four pence.

Ranking numbers

In your assessment you may be required to rank numbers in order of size. The order of ranking could be specified as ascending or descending size.

Let's consider an example:

The table below describes Jazz Co's bank balance at the end of each of the last four months.

January	February	March	April
£	£	£	£
1,209.89	980.42	4,654.68	3,452.34

You may need to rank these balances in **ascending order**. This would mean that you start with the smallest value.

Month	£
February	980.42
January	1,209.89
April	3,452.34
March	4,654.68

If you are asked to rank in **descending order** you would start with the largest number.

Month	£
March	4,654.68
April	3,452.34
January	1,209.89
February	980.42

So far the balance at the end of each month has been positive. You may also come across negative values and have to include these in a ranking.

Jazz Co's bank balance goes into overdraft (effectively a negative bank balance) for the next two months, so the month-end balances are as follows:

January	February	March	April	May	June
£	£	£	£	£	£
1,209.89	980.42	4,654.68	3,452.34	– 1,983.21	– 867.32

Negative numbers may also be shown as numbers in brackets. This is particularly common in accounting information.

January	February	March	April	May	June
£	£	£	£	£	£
1,209.89	980.42	4,654.68	3,452.34	(1,983.21)	(867.32)

One thing you need to be careful with when dealing with negative numbers is that a large negative number is a lower value. So Jazz's month-end balance in May is a lower number than June. So if we rank the month-end values for all six months in ascending order we start with the lowest value, which is May:

Month	£
May	(1,983.21)
June	(867.32)
February	980.42
January	1,209.89
April	3,452.34
March	4,654.68

Calculating increases and decreases

In your assessment you could be asked to calculate a change between two numbers. For example you could be asked to calculate the increase or decrease in Jazz's bank balance each month. To calculate the change you need to subtract the previous month's balance from the month-end balance for each-month as shown below (figures in brackets are a decrease):

	January	February	March	April	May	June
	£	£	£	£	£	£
Balance	1,209.89	980.42	4,654.68	3,452.34	(1,983.21)	(867.32)
Change	Note	(229.47)	3,674.26	(1,202.34)	(5,435.55)	1,115.89

Note. We cannot calculate the change for January as we have not been provided with a figure for the previous month.

You need to be particularly careful when a calculation includes a negative figure. For example the change in June is (£867.32) – (£1,983.21) = £1,115.89. You must be careful to enter the values into your calculator as negative numbers or you will not get the correct answer.

Calculating a range

Another task you may be asked to perform in your assessment is to calculate the range for a series of numbers. This is similar to calculating the change in two numbers that we just looked at. The range is the difference (or change) between the lowest and highest values in a series.

> **KEYWORD**
>
> Range = Highest value – Lowest value

The range of Jazz's month-end balances is £4,654.68 – (£1,983.21) = £6,637.89.

You could check this is correct by adding the range to the lowest value to get the highest value.

Lowest value + Range = Highest value

(£1,983.21) + £6,637.89 = £4,654.68

Rounding numbers

It is not always necessary to provide numerical information in full detail. In your assessment you could be asked to round to the nearest whole number or to two decimal places.

The number of pence in each month-end balance is unlikely to be important for any business decisions relying on this information. Therefore, it may be more convenient to reduce the detail by rounding. You could be asked to identify Jazz's highest month-end balance to the nearest £ (the nearest whole number).

When rounding to the nearest whole number you must apply the following rule:

> **Rounding rule (1 decimal place)**
>
> If the digit to the immediate right of the decimal point is 4, 3, 2 or 1, **simply drop all digits that come after the decimal point.**
>
> If the digit to the immediate right of the decimal point is 5, 6, 7, 8 or 9, **add one to the digit immediately before the decimal point, and drop all digits to the right of it.**

> **Example**
> 1) We apply this to the highest balance of £4,654.68 the digit to the right of the decimal point is 6.
> 2) We then add 1 to the digit before the decimal point and drop all numbers after the decimal point.
> 3) Finally, the highest value rounded to the **nearest £** (whole number) is £4,655.

Alternatively, you could be asked to round a value with more decimal places to two decimal places (equivalent to the nearest penny).

You could be asked to calculate half of the lowest monthly balance to **two decimal places**.

> **Rounding rule (2 decimal places)**
>
> If the digit to the immediate right of the second decimal place is 4, 3, 2 or 1, **simply drop all digits that come after the second decimal place.**
>
> If the digit to the immediate right of the second decimal place is 5, 6, 7, 8 or 9, **add one to the second decimal place, and drop all digits to the right of it.**

Example

Half of the lowest balance is (£1,983.21) ÷ 2 = (£991.605).

To round this to two decimal places is a similar process to rounding to the nearest whole number, except that you start with the second number after the decimal point which is known as the second decimal place. So the rule for rounding to two decimal places is as follows.

Applying this rule to the result we calculated for half of the lowest balance we get £991.61.

2 Using a calculator

Working with numbers in a business environment, it is important for you to be familiar with a calculator and how it works. Calculators can be simple or complicated, but the basic functions that you will use in this assessment will be the same.

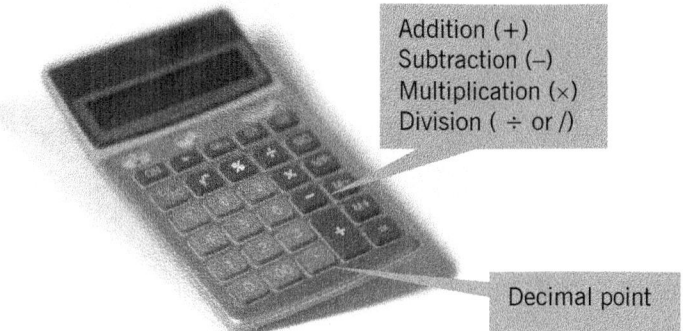

Addition (+)
Subtraction (−)
Multiplication (×)
Division (÷ or /)

Decimal point

3 Addition and subtraction

In your assessment, you will be required to add numbers, both whole numbers and numbers with one or two decimal places.

Money is usually shown to two decimal places, as the numbers before the decimal point indicate the pounds and the numbers after the decimal point indicate the pence.

You may be presented with numbers in columns and have to total them.

How it works

	20,001.20
	10,020.10
	5,200.05
	2,005.02
Total	37,226.37

To add the figures together to come to the total in the shaded box, you should:

1. Enter the first figure carefully into your calculator
2. Press the + button
3. Enter the second figure
4. Press the + button
5. Enter the third figure
6. Press the + button
7. Enter the fourth figure
8. Press the = button

> Ensure you enter figures carefully into your calculator, including the decimal point, or you may make an error.

Try this on the sum above and see if your answer matches ours.

In your assessment, you will be required to subtract or 'take away' numbers, both whole numbers and numbers with one or two decimal places.

TASK 1 **(a)** Your organisation keeps detailed records of expenses. Motor fuel expenses for each of four delivery vehicles are shown in the table below.

Complete the table to show the total expense for motor fuel.

Delivery vehicles	Motor fuel expense
	£
Vehicle 1	128.42
Vehicle 2	196.55
Vehicle 3	86.09
Vehicle 4	112.42
Total	

(b) **Complete the table to show the expense for envelopes.** (**Note.** You may need to do this in two steps in a separate working, as shown above.)

Stationery items	Expense
	£
Ink tanks	37.50
Printer paper	18.39

Stationery items	Expense
	£
Envelopes	
Pens	7.23
Total	**104.03**

(c) Last year your organisation recorded income and expenses as shown in the table below:

Expenses	£
Goods for resale	149,000
Wages	26,800
Office expenses	14,600
Selling expenses	19,100

Use the income and expenses figures to complete the following calculations.

Calculate total expenses.

£ ☐

4 Multiplication and division

In your assessment you could be required to multiply or divide any two numbers, which could be a mixture of whole numbers or numbers with one or two decimal places.

If your answer comes to more than two decimal places, you will need to apply 'rounding', to two decimal places. As we saw in section 1 of this chapter rounding to two decimal places involves leaving off all the numbers after the second decimal place in your answer. All you have to remember is that, if the number in the third decimal place in your calculation is 5 or higher, you should increase the number in the second decimal place by 1.

How it works

For example, if your answer is 25.52384, you would present this as 25.52.

If your answer is 25.52684, you would present this as 25.53.

You are likely to be told that an organisation has bought a number of items at a unit price, and to work out the total price. To do this, you must multiply the price by the number of items purchased.

How it works

Your organisation purchased 5 ink cartridges at £24.95 per cartridge from Combes Stationers. **What is the total cost of the ink cartridges?**

To calculate this sum on your calculator, you should:

1. Enter the cost figure, which is 24.95
2. Press the × button
3. Enter the number of cartridges purchased, which is 5
4. Press the = button
5. The screen will now show the total cost of £124.75 for the ink cartridges

Alternatively, you could be told that an organisation has bought a number of items at a total price, and be asked to work out the unit price. To do this, you must divide the total price by the number of items purchased.

How it works

Your organisation purchased 30 reams of paper from Office Suppliers, for a total cost of £74.40. **What is the unit price of one ream of paper?**

To calculate this sum on your calculator, you should:

1. Enter the total cost figure, which is 74.4
2. Press the ÷ button
3. Enter the number of reams purchased, which is 30
4. Press the = button
5. The screen will now show the unit price of a ream of paper of £2.48

TASK 2 Your organisation purchased 12 bottles of hand soap at £1.25 per bottle from Discount Suppliers.

(a) **What is the total cost of the hand soap?**

£ [   ]

Your organisation purchased 12 towels from Discount Suppliers, with a total cost of £52.56.

(b) **What is the unit price of a towel?**

£ [   ]

5 Calculations with time

In your assessment you may be asked to perform calculations involving common units of time. For instance, you could be asked to calculate how long a task takes or how much time is available.

Let's consider how this should be applied to the following examples.

How it works

Use the following information to calculate how many man hours it takes Singh Tyres Ltd to produce each tyre:

Sing tyres produces 8,000 tyres in one week.

It employs 220 staff in the tyre production process.

Each employee works a five-day week and works eight hours per day.

Solution:

First you need to establish the total number of man hours used in the week's production:

5 × 8 × 220 = 8,800 hours.

You then need to divide this number of hours by the number of tyres produced:

8,800 ÷ 8,000 = **1.1 hours.**

How it works

The total number of working days in December in the production department is 17. Each working day is 7.5 hours. Calculate the number of free production days in December given the following jobs already scheduled.

Provide your answer to the nearest day.

Job	Items to be produced	Time per item
A	100	0.5 hours
B	20	1.3 hours

To answer this you first have to calculate the total committed production time:

(100 × 0.5) + (20 × 1.3) = 76 hours.

You then need to deduct this from the total production time in December. However, before you do this calculation you need to have both figures expressed in the same units. So you need the total number of hours of production time in December:

17 × 7.5 = 127.5 hours.

Now you can deduct the committed production time:

127.5 − 76 = 51.5 hours.

You were asked to provide the answer to the nearest day (remember a working day is stated as 7.5 hours:

51.5 ÷ 7.5 = 6.86 = 7 days.

What these examples show is that you may have some extra stages in calculations related to time periods connected to changing the units in which numbers are expressed. Two common reasons for this are:

- Putting your answer into the units in which you were asked to express the answer
- Expressing two time periods in the same terms before performing addition or subtraction

6 Ratios

In your assessment, you may have to calculate the ratio of one whole number to another whole number. A ratio will be presented as 'a whole number: a whole number', for example, 3 : 1. This is a way of expressing mathematically that the first number is three times bigger than the second number.

KEYWORD

A **ratio** compares values. A ratio will show how much of one thing is compared to another.

How it works

You may be given a list of costs (for example, stationery items, below), and asked what the ratio of one item to the total or to another item is. You may be given a range of ratios and asked which the correct one is, as shown below.

Stationery items	Expense £
Ink tanks	25.00
Printer paper	13.29
Envelopes	15.11
Pens	21.60
Total	75.00

Which of the following is the ratio of the total expense for stationery items to the expense for ink tanks?

- 2:1
- 3:1
- 4:1

To calculate this, divide the total expense by the expense of ink tanks. On your calculator, you should:

1. Enter the total expense figure, which is 75
2. Press the ÷ button
3. Enter the figure for ink tanks, which is 25
4. Press the = button
5. This gives the answer 3, so the ratio is 3:1. In other words, the total expense is three times bigger than the cost of ink tanks.

TASK 3 Your organisation has the following costs relating to light and heat.

	£
Light	200,000
Heat	100,000
Total	300,000

Which of the following is the ratio of the total cost for light and heat to the cost for heat?

Options:

2:1
3:1
4:1

7 Proportions as fractions

In your assessment you might be required to calculate the proportion of one whole number to another whole number and the answer might result in a fraction. This is an expression of the relationship between the two numbers, for example, that directors' salaries equal half of total salary costs for an organisation.

> **KEYWORDS**
>
> A **fraction** is a number that represents an equal part of a whole, for example there are four equal slices in one cake, so the fraction is 1/4 of the cake.
>
> A **decimal** is another way of writing a fraction (1/4 is the same as 0.25)
>
> The **factor** is a number which divides exactly into another number
>
> **Numerator** is the top number in a fraction
>
> **Denominator** is the bottom number in a fraction

How it works

You could be given the costs for the same items as above and asked what proportion of total stationery costs the ink tanks are.

Stationery items	Expense
	£
Ink tanks	20.00
Printer paper	13.29
Envelopes	25.11
Pens	21.60
Total stationery costs	80.00

As the amount for ink tanks is smaller than the total stationery costs, the answer is going to be a fraction. This fraction would be presented initially as $\frac{20}{80}$. However, fractions should always be presented in the smallest numbers possible (this is often referred to as 'simplifying').

> **Steps:**
>
> 1 Find a number that **both numbers** in the fraction can be divided by.
>
> In simple cases, the bottom number will be divisible by the top number (which means you will be able to divide the bottom number by the top number and the answer will be a whole number). This is the **FACTOR.**
>
> 2 Using the factor, divide both numbers (the top (numerator) and the bottom (denominator)).
>
> 3 This will give you your fraction.

In the following example, we apply the steps above.

Example

1   Take the initial fraction $\frac{20}{80}$

2 Determine whether the bottom number can be divided by the top number *(in this case, the number can be divided by 20 so it is the **factor**)*
3 Enter 80 into the calculator
4 Press the ÷ button
5 Enter 20 into the calculator *(as you worked out from part (2))*
6 Press the = button
7 The calculator displays 4

In this instance, the **bottom number is divisible by the top number**. This can be presented as follows:

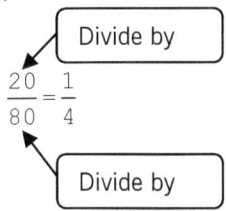

The answer is therefore $\frac{1}{4}$

In the exam you could be expected to calculate the following simple fractions:

- $\frac{1}{2}$

- $\frac{1}{4}$

- $\frac{1}{5}$

- $\frac{1}{10}$

TASK 4 Your organisation has the following costs for catering supplies.

	£
Tea	75
Coffee	250
Milk	425
Total	750

Calculate the fraction of tea costs to the total costs.

8 Percentages

In your assessment, you may be required to calculate what percentage one figure is of another. The answer may be a whole number, or a number to one or two decimal places.

> **KEYWORDS**
>
> A **percentage (%)** is a fraction with a denominator of 100. It tells you how many parts per 100 there are.

Example

'75% of the population drinks tea'.

What this means is that out of every 100 people in the population, 75 of them drink tea. Accordingly, 25 of them don't, so you could also say that 25% of the population does not drink tea.

Calculating a percentage in this way can give more user-friendly information than if you were told that the population is 61,792,000, of which 46,344,000 drink tea.

In the same way, it might be more useful for directors of an organisation to be told that, for every £100 earned, £25 is profit (25%) – rather than just being told that for total income of £37,794,584, profit is £9,448,646.

How it works

You might be given figures for sales and expense, for example:

	£
Sales	120,000
Expenses	90,000
Profit (Sales less expenses)	30,000

You may then be asked to calculate profit as a percentage of sales. To calculate this on your calculator, you should:

1. Enter the profit figure, which is 30,000
2. Press the ÷ button
3. Enter the sales figure, which is 120,000
4. Press the = button
5. The screen should show a figure after the decimal place, 0.25
6. Press the × button
7. Enter 100

8   Press the = button
9   The screen will show the percentage figure (in this case, 25%). In other words, for every £100 earned, the organisation makes £25 profit.

Alternatively, you may be given a figure (for example, a sales price) and be told that it is going to increase by a certain percentage. You may be asked what the amount of the increase is.

How it works

You might be told that the sales price for Part AB23 is £4.80 and that it is going to increase by 5%. You could be required to calculate the amount of the rise.

The best way to understand this is to say that £4.80 is 100%. You can calculate what 1% is by dividing the price by 100. You can then find 5% by multiplying by 5. To calculate the figure, you therefore need to:

1   Enter the existing price, which is 4.80
2   Press the ÷ button
3   Enter 100
4   Press the = button
5   The screen shows 1%, which is 0.048
6   Press the × button
7   Enter 5
8   Press the = button
9   The screen shows 5%, which is 0.24

The increase is 24 pence (you would show this in the assessment as £0.24).

TASK 5 (a) Your organisation has produced the following figures for the year.

	£
Sales	253,700
Expenses	190,275
Profit (sales less expenses)	63,425

Calculate profit as a percentage of sales.

[   ] %

(b) The current selling price of part DC45IT is £569. This is going to increase by 3%.
Calculate the increase in the selling price to the nearest penny.

£ [   ]

9 Fractions

You might be asked to apply a fraction to a whole number. This may give an answer which is a whole number, or a number to one or two decimal places.

> **Exam Focus Point**
>
> A previous Examiner's Report stated that many students struggled with calculating fractional increases and decimal increases (however, they were competent at calculating percentage increases). Make sure you can calculate these increases and decreases using decimals and fractions, and that you can calculate the new prices when percentage increases have been applied. Pay close attention to the next example for the method.

How it works

You might be told the current selling price of an item and be told that it is going to rise by a fraction. For example, the current selling price of part AX345 is £36. It is going to rise by $\frac{1}{6}$. What is the increase in selling price for part AX345?

To calculate this figure on your calculator, you need to:

1. Enter the existing price, which is 36
2. Press the × button
3. Enter the top number in the fraction, which is 1
4. Press the ÷ button
5. Enter the bottom number in the fraction, which is 6
6. Press the = button
7. The screen shows the increase in the selling price, which is 6

Steps 2 and 3 are NOT absolutely necessary when the top number of the fraction is 1, but are necessary if the top number is higher than 1, for example where the fraction is 2/3.

TASK 6 (a) The current selling price of part XZ20 is £49. This is going to increase by $\frac{1}{4}$.

Calculate the increase in the selling price.

£ ⬜

(b) The current selling price of part CVB34 is £25. This is going to increase by $\frac{1}{5}$.

Calculate the increase in the selling price.

£ ⬜

10 Converting percentages, fractions and decimals

The relationship between two values can be expressed as either a fraction, a decimal or a percentage. Your assessment questions may require you to convert a value expressed one way into another form – for instance converting a fraction such as ½ into a percentage (50%) or a decimal (0.5).

Percentages, fractions and decimals are different ways of expressing the same thing. One per cent is $\frac{1}{100}$ as a fraction and 0.01 as a decimal. We can use this fact to convert between the different ways to express a value.

Fractions and percentages

If you are asked to convert a percentage into a fraction, for example 25%, first convert this to a number of hundredths: $\frac{25}{100}$. Then divide the top number into the bottom one, 100 ÷ 25 = 4. This is the bottom of the fraction and the top will be 1, giving $\frac{1}{4}$.

To convert a fraction into a percentage divide the bottom of the fraction into 100. So, to convert $\frac{1}{5}$ into a percentage, 100 ÷ 5 = 20%.

Percentage and decimals

In a decimal value the first two decimal places equate to a number of hundredths. The 0.25 could be described as twenty-five hundredths. We already know that percentages are just hundredths, so 0.25 is equal to 25%. You just need to multiply the decimal by 100:

0.25 × 100 = 25%.

It is equally easy to convert in the opposite direction. You simply need to divide the percentage to get a decimal.

250% is 250 ÷ 100 = 2.5

Decimals and fractions

To convert a decimal to a fraction first multiply by 100 then divide the result into 100. If this gives a whole number then this is the bottom of the fraction with 1 on the top. For example if you need to convert 0.2 into a fraction, multiply by 100: 0.2 × 100 = 20.

Divide this result into 100, 100 ÷ 20 = 5.

The fraction is $\frac{1}{5}$.

To convert a fraction into a decimal divide the bottom of the fraction into 100, then divide by 100. Using $\frac{1}{5}$,

$100 \div 5 = 20$

$20 \div 100 = 0.2$.

In order to get comfortable with converting between these ways of presenting numerical information you need to practise as many examples as possible.

TASK 7 A company has the following types of expenditure.

Expense	£
Selling	2,300
Distribution	11,500
Administration	9,200

Calculate the proportion of total expenditure made up of selling expenses. Express your answer as a:

Fraction

Decimal

Percentage

11 Averages

In your assessment, you may have to calculate the average value. An average gives an indication of typical values in a series of numbers. There are two averages which you need to be able to calculate. They are the **mean** and the **mode.**

Exam Focus Point

In a previous Examiner's Report, students did not always understand the meaning of mean and mode, nor could they apply it to the question. Ensure you are familiar with the terms and practise your questions.

> **KEYWORDS**
>
> The **mean** is a set of data whereby the TOTAL of the values is divided by the NUMBER of values. This is often referred to as calculating the **average** of a range.
>
> The **mode** is the value that occurs the most often.

Mean (Average)

The mean that you calculate may be a whole number or a decimal which you could also be asked to round. The mean cost of five units, for instance, is the total cost divided by the number of elements making up that cost (5); that is what the individual unit cost would be if they were all the same. It is critical therefore to work out how many elements make up the total, in order to do the calculation.

How it works

You may be given a range of costs, with a total, and asked what the mean average cost is. For example, the following are the costs of wages per department in your organisation. There are four elements (departments) making up the total cost.

	£
Department 1	253,049
Department 2	645,900
Department 3	234,984
Department 4	302,845
Total	1,436,778

To calculate the average cost per department on your calculator, you need to:

1. Enter the total cost, which is £1,436,778
2. Press the ÷ button
3. Enter the total number of departments being averaged (in this case 4)
4. Press the = button
5. The screen should show the average cost per department, which is £359,194.50

The key thing to remember when calculating the mean is that the number you divide by is the number of things being averaged. This will never be more than 5 in your assessment, but could be 2, 3 or 4.

If you had been asked for the average to the nearest whole number you would need to apply rounding.

The number to the right of the decimal point is 5. Following the rule for rounding covered earlier in this chapter you must add 1 number before the decimal point, and drop the digits after the decimal point.

This gives an answer of £359,195.

TASK 8 The following table shows the number of miles driven by the three delivery vehicles belonging to your organisation during the year:

Delivery vehicles	Mileage
	£
Vehicle 1	2,645
Vehicle 2	1,035
Vehicle 3	895
Total	4,575

Calculate the average number of miles driven by the delivery vehicles.

☐ miles

Mode

The mode is a different type of average. The mode is the **most frequently occurring value**. As an example assume the following series of values is the number of out-of-stock customer orders in a week:

Week 1	7
Week 2	0
Week 3	3
Week 4	3
Week 5	4
Week 6	8
Week 7	4
Week 8	1
Week 9	3
Week 10	11

Looking at this information you can see that there are three weeks when the number of stockouts is 3. This is the most commonly occurring value and so it is the mode.

The mode is not necessarily just one value. If the number of stockouts in week 10 had been 4 rather than 11 the mode would be 3 and 4. This is an important difference to the mean which is always a single value, although not necessarily one that was actually recorded. The mean number of stockout is 4.4, but you can see that there was not a week when 4.4 stockouts were experienced.

> **Exam Focus Point**
>
> Another weakness identified by a previous Examiner's Report was that "students were not able to use estimation". It is essential you read the question carefully and understand what it is asking you to calculate.

Using averages to estimate a value

One use of averages is to estimate another value. For instance, if you know the **mean value** of sales for one month you could **estimate** the value of sales for the year by multiplying the monthly sales by 12.

The mode can also be used to predict a value. For instance, if the mode for the number of hours of overtime worked by an employee per day over the last 30 days is 1.5 hours, this can be seen as the most likely value for the next day.

How it works

The following is the number of invoices sent out by the finance department per day for the last 5 business days together with the number of invoice queries received from customers:

	Monday	Tuesday	Wednesday	Thursday	Friday
Number of invoices	120	142	111	98	145
Number of queries	4	5	2	4	4

Estimate the number of invoices that the finance department will produce in the next 20 business days.

The daily mean can be used to estimate the number of invoices over a number of days.

Daily mean = (120 + 142 + 111 + 98 + 145) ÷ 5 = 123.2.

Estimate for 20 days 123.2 × 20 = **2,464**.

Estimate the most likely number of queries that the finance department will receive on the next business day.

The mode is the most likely value to occur = 4.

12 Presenting numerical data

The vast majority of people who work in a financial environment are required to use spreadsheets to perform their duties. In your exam you may be examined on using formulas as well as using tools to enhance the presentation of your information

Using formulas

In most spreadsheets the contents of any cell can be one of the following:

	Description
Text	A text cell usually contains words. Numbers that do not represent numeric values for calculation purposes (eg a part number) may be entered in a way that tells Excel to treat the cell contents as text. To do this, enter an apostrophe before the number: '451, for example.
Values	A value is a number that can be used in a calculation.
Formulas	A formula refers to other cells in the spreadsheet and performs some type of computation with them.

In **Microsoft Excel**, formulas start with the equals sign =, followed by the elements to be calculated (the operands) and the calculation operators (such as +, -, /, *).

Formulas can be used to perform a variety of calculations. Here are some examples:

	Description
Addition	=C4+5
	This formula adds 5 to the value in C4. The result will appear in the cell holding the formula.
	=C4+C5
	This formula adds the value in C4 to the value in C5. The result will appear in the cell holding the formula.
	=sum(C4:C8)
	This formula adds all of the contents of cells C4 to C8. The result will appear in the cell holding the formula.
Subtraction	=C4-5
	This formula subtracts 5 from the value in C4. The result will appear in the cell holding the formula.
	=C4-C5
	This formula subtracts the value in C5 from the value in C4. The result will appear in the cell holding the formula.

	Description
Multiplication	=C4*5 This formula multiplies the value in C4 by 5. The result will appear in the cell holding the formula. =C4*C5 This formula multiplies the value in C4 by the value in C5. The result will appear in the cell holding the formula.
Division	=C4/5 This formula divides the value in C4 by 5. The result will appear in the cell holding the formula. =C4/C5 This formula divides the value in C4 by the value in C5. The result will appear in the cell holding the formula.
Combinations	= C4+C5-C6 Spreadsheets allow combinations of the formula to be made in individual combinations. The formula adds the value of C5 to the value in C4 and then subtracts the value in C6.

Tools to enhance the presentation of your information

Most spreadsheets enable the **formatting of contents of cells**. In most cases this is achieved by highlighting the cells that you wish to be formatted and then selecting the relevant option. In most cases, a cell can have **multiple formats** applied, so for example, the contents of a cell might be made bold and the colour changed to blue. The symbols in the table below are taken from Excel.

	Symbol	Description
Bold	B	123456.789 Makes the contents of a cell stand out.
Italics	I	123456.789 Adds a slant to the contents of a cell.
Underline	U	123456.789 Adds a line under the contents of a cell.

	Symbol	Description
Font colour	A ▾	123456.789 Changes the colour of the contents of a cell.
Font style and size	Calibri ▾ 11 ▾	123456.8 The font format and size of the contents of a cell are changed.
Fill cell	🎨 ▾	123456.789 The background colour to the cell is changed.
Accounting	💲 ▾	$ 123,456.79 The contents of a cell are presented in a number of different ways, such as changing the currency of the numbers.
Thousands	,	123,456.79 Adds a comma into a number to indicate thosands.
Percentages	%	12345679% Displays the contents of a cell as a percentage.
Decimal places	←.0 .00 .00 →0	123456.78900 123456.8 Increases and decreases the number of decimal places a number is shown to.

Exam Focus Point

In your exam, be prepared to combine your knowledge of spreadsheets with your other studies on numbers. For example, you could be asked to format the highest and lowest values in a spreadsheet in a particular colour.

TASK 9 Write a spreadsheet formula that will add cells C3, C4, C5 and C6 into C7. Then write another formula that multiplies the answer by the total in C8.

	1st formula
	2nd formula

Chapter overview

Working with numbers in the business environment may involve recording values in words or figures.

Your assessment may require you to rank a series of numbers in ascending or descending order, as well as calculate increases and decreases.

You may be required to apply rounding to your answers to assessment questions either to two decimal places or to the nearest whole number.

You need to be confident in the use of a calculator to perform basic mathematical functions on data provided in questions. Ensure that you enter figures carefully into your calculator, including the decimal point, or you may make an error.

Money is usually shown to two decimal places, as the numbers before the decimal point indicate the pounds and the numbers after the decimal point indicate the pence.

If you are working with units of time make sure that you provide your answer in the correct units and always perform subtraction and addition with numbers expressed in the same units.

In your assessment, you may have to express one value in terms of another. This can be done using ratios, decimals, fractions or percentages.

You may also be required to convert between these different ways of expressing the relationship between two values – for instance converting a fraction such as ½ into a percentage (50%) or a decimal (0.5).

There are two averages you may be required to calculate: the mean, which is the total of all values divided by the number of values, and the mode, which is the most frequently occurring value in a series of numbers.

In your assessment, you may need to use an average to predict or estimate a future value.

Most spreadsheet software enables the use of formulas. These allow calculations, such as adding, subtracting, multiplying, and dividing to be performed quickly and consistently.

The contents of spreadsheet cells can be formatted in several different ways. Multiple formats can be used on the same cell.

Keywords

A **DECIMAL** is another way of writing a fraction (1/4 is the same as 0.25)

DENOMINATOR is the bottom number in a fraction

The **FACTOR** is a number which divides exactly into another number

In a spreadsheet, a **FORMULA** refers to other cells in the spreadsheet and performs some type of computation with them.

A **FRACTION** is a number that represents a part of a whole; for example there are four slices in one cake, so the fraction is 1/4 of the cake.

The **MEAN** is a set of data whereby the TOTAL of the values is divided by the NUMBER of values. This is often referred to as calculating the **AVERAGE** of a range.

The **MODE** is the value that occurs the most often

NUMERATOR is the top number in a fraction

A **PERCENTAGE** (%) is a fraction with a denominator of 100. It tells you how many parts per 100 there are.

RANGE = Highest value – Lowest value

A **RATIO** compares values. A ratio will show how much of one thing is compared to another.

In a spreadsheet, a **VALUE** is a number that can be used in a calculation.

4 Using numbers in business: Test your learning

This chapter gives you question practice on the topics you covered in the previous chapter. The questions are in the same style you can expect in your assessment. You can find the answers at the back of this Workbook.

1   Your organisation sold two cars for a total of £958.30 to Super Car Traders.

   (a) **What is the average price of each car?**

   £ [   ]

   A third car is sold for £1200.

   (b) **What is the revised total value of sales?**

   £ [   ]

   (c) **What percentage of total sales does the sale of the third car represent? Work to the nearest percentage point.**

   [   ] %

2   An organisation is reviewing the selling price of some of its products.

   The current selling price of product number 52 is £17.00. This is to be increased by $\frac{1}{5}$ (one fifth).

   (a) **Calculate the increase in selling price for product number 52:**

   £ [   ]

   The current selling price of product number 12 is £18.00. This is to be increased by 6%.

(b) Calculate the increase in selling price for product number 12:

£ ☐

3 An organisation is reviewing the selling price of some of its products.

The current selling price of product number 104 is £62. This is to be increased by $\frac{1}{10}$.

(a) Calculate the increase in selling price for product number 104:

£ ☐

The current selling price of product number AZ25 is £9. This is to be increased by 7.5%. Provide your answer to the nearest penny.

(b) Calculate the increase in selling price for product number AZ25:

£ ☐

4 Your organisation keeps detailed records of sales.

Sales at each of four outlets are shown in the table below.

(a) Complete the table to show the sales at Outlet 4:

Sales per outlet	£
Outlet 1	250,368.25
Outlet 2	199,473.79
Outlet 3	302,699.39
Outlet 4	
Total	1,127,751.60

(b) Calculate the average sales per outlet:

£ ☐

Analysed sales at Outlet 1 are shown in the table below.

(c) **Complete the table to show the sales from menswear:**

Item	£
Menswear	
Ladieswear	61,506
Childrenswear	62,595
Household fabrics	50,076
Total	250,380

(d) **Which of the following is the ratio of total sales at Outlet 1 to sales of childrenswear at Outlet 1?**

- 4:1
- 5:1
- 6:1

(e) **Which of the following is the percentage of the total sales at Outlet 1 made up by household fabrics?**

- 20%
- 16.67%
- 14.29%

5 Your organisation keeps detailed records of costs.

Costs at each of two premises are shown in the table below.

(a) **Complete the table to show the costs at Premises 2:**

Costs per premises	£
Premises 1	50,924.72
Premises 2	
Total	102,049.94

(b) **Calculate the average cost for each premises:**

£ ☐

Analysed costs at Premises 1 are shown in the table below.

Item	£
Cost of sales	34,368
Distribution costs	6,372
Administration costs	10,185
Total	50,925

(c) Which of the following is the ratio of total costs to administration costs?

- 4:1
- 5:1
- 6:1

(d) Express your answer to (c) as a percentage:

 %

6 You have been given the following spreadsheet to complete.

	A	B	C	D
1	Month	UK sales	Overseas sales	Total UK and overseas sales
2		£	£	£
3	January	18,692	289,642	
4	February		249,875	275,896
5	Total		539,517	

(a) In cell D3, use an appropriate formula to calculate the total sales figure for January.

(b) In cell B4, use an appropriate formula to calculate the UK sales figure for February.

(c) In cell B5, use an appropriate formula to calculate the total UK sales figure.

(d) In cell D5, use an appropriate formula to calculate the total UK and overseas sales figure.

(e) **Which of the following button would you select to change the background colour of a cell?**

 ☐

 ☐

 ☐

 ☐

Chapter tasks: answers

Chapter tasks: answers

Chapter 1

Task 1

A travel agent — Services

A maker of musical instruments — Manufacturing

An online bookseller — Retail

Task 2

Ensuring the manufacturing process within a factory is maintained — Production

Producing an employment contract for new staff — Human resources

Producing budgets for management — Finance

Task 3

Informing the team leader that you have found the task assigned to you difficult and that you are falling behind schedule. Team working is not just offering to help others, but also to highlight when you are having issues yourself and calling on the team to help you.

Task 4

The order of priority is:

B	A	C

It is important to prioritise key work before administration, so in this case, complete the estimates before updating the filing. As the deadline for the material usage is later, then this can be worked on last of all of these three tasks.

Task 5

(ii)

(i) describes adaptability. (iii) describes commitment and (iv) describes confidentiality (which is an example of professional behaviour). Being honest is not only being truthful, but also being straightforward and transparent in your dealings and relationships.

Task 6

Notifying a customer who has failed to pay an invoice that you intend to take legal action. — **Letter**

Asking the sales department for the total of last week's sales. — **Email**

Discussing job performance with an employee. — **Face-to-face**

Internal communication can usually be made via email, unless it is of a sensitive or confidential nature, such as a job review or issue regarding pay. External communication which is of a serious nature, such as chasing payment should be made by letter (and likely to be sent by registered mail to guarantee that the recipient has received it).

Task 7

AmirS	☐
PASSWORD	☐
Computer	☐
@mirS1ngh23	✓

Passwords should be complex and not use words or sequences.

Task 8

Expenses
advertising cost
insurance
fuel costs
interest on a bank overdraft
wages and salaries

Income
sale
interest received

Task 9

Cash sale	Credit sale
Sale of goods when cash is paid on delivery.	Sale of goods when payment is made at a date later than delivery.
Sale of services when cash is paid on delivery of the service.	Sale of services when cash is paid at a date later than the service was provided.
Cash purchase	**Credit purchase**
Purchase of goods when payment is made at the same time as delivery of the goods.	Purchase of goods when payment is made at a date later than delivery.
Purchase of services when payment is made at the same time as the service is provided.	Purchase of a service when payment is made at a later date than the service is provided.

Task 10

(a) When income exceeds expenditure, an organisation has made a profit ✓

(b) When expenditure exceeds income, an organisation has made a loss ✓

(c) Reducing the period of time before customers have to pay ✓

(d) The ability to increase investment in the business ✓

(e)

Organisation	Profit	Loss
Organisation A	✓	
Organisation B	✓	

Task 11

A delivery note should state the purchase order number. ✓

Task 12

(a) The purchase order number ✓

(b) The invoice amount should be queried with the supplier. ✓

Chapter 3

Task 1

(a)

Delivery vehicles	Motor fuel expense
	£
Vehicle 1	128.42
Vehicle 2	196.55
Vehicle 3	86.09
Vehicle 4	112.42
Total	**523.48**

(b)

Stationery items	Expense
	£
Ink tanks	37.50
Printer paper	18.39
Envelopes	40.91
Pens	7.23
Total	**104.03**

(c) Total expenditure = £149,000 + £26,800 + £14,600 + £19,100

£ | 209,500 |

Task 2

(a) The total cost of the hand soap = 12 × £1.25

£ | 15 |

(b) The unit price of a towel = £52.56 ÷ 12

£ | 4.38 |

Task 3

The ratio of the total cost for light and heat to the cost for heat

The total cost for light and heat is 300,000

The cost heat is 100,000

The calculation is 300,000: 100,000

Which can be simplified as 3~~00,000~~: 1~~00,000~~

> 3:1

Task 4

Calculate the fraction of tea costs to total costs:

1. Tea costs = 75

   Total costs = 750

2. $\dfrac{75}{750}$

3. The FACTOR in this case is 75, as 75 will divide into the top number (numerator) once and the bottom number (denominator) ten times.

   > $\dfrac{1}{10}$

   One tenth of the total costs represents the costs of tea.

Task 5

(a) Profit as a percentage of sales = £63,425 ÷ £253,700 × 100

> 25 %

(b) The increase in the selling price = £569 ÷ 100 × 3

> £ 17.07

Task 6

(a) The increase in the selling price = £49 ÷ 4

> £ 12.25

(b) The increase in the selling price = £25 ÷ 5

> £ 5

Task 7

Fraction

(£11,500 + £9,200 + £2,300) ÷ £2,300

$$\frac{1}{10}$$

Decimal

100 ÷ 10 ÷ 100

| 0.1 |

Percentage

0.1 × 100

| 10 | %

Task 8

The average number of miles driven by the delivery vehicles = 4,575 ÷ 3

| 1,525 | miles

Task 9

Formula to be entered in c7 that adds cells C3, C4, C5 and C6. =sum(c3:c6) Or =c3+c4+c5+c5

Formula that multiplies the total in c7 by the total in C8. =c7*c8

Test your learning: answers

Test your learning: answers

Chapter 2

1. (a) A sole trader is a **private sector** organisation.

   (b) The police service **does not** aim to make a profit.

2. (a) Detailed expenditure analysis provided by the finance department of a partnership is used by the general public to make business decisions.

   False ✓

   Detailed expenditure will be used in the management meetings (management accounts); only statutory financial statements will be made available to the public and these vary in the level of detail according to the size of the company.

   (b) An organisation's IT department provides a service to customers and suppliers.

   False ✓

   An organisation's IT department will assist the employees of the company not external parties.

3. Information about pay increases held on the computer should be kept

   in a password-protected file with access restricted to those who need the information.

   A supplier of the organisation where you work asks you who the main customers of the organisation are. You reply:

   'I am sorry but I cannot give you any information as it is confidential.'

4 Frequently arriving late for work is fine if it is because your train is late.

False ✓

It would be recommended that you catch an earlier train as it appears that you are not leaving sufficient leeway or time for your travel to the workplace.

Use of personal phones at work is acceptable provided that you leave the office to avoid disturbing colleagues.

False ✓

Personal communication is preferably kept to a minimum in the workplace as you have a job to do.

5 (a) Communicating by letter is **appropriate** for communications when **speed** is not of the highest importance.

(b) Teams work best when members are given clear goals by the team leader.

True ✓

Giving team members unrealistic deadlines will ensure that they work harder.

False ✓

Making deadlines unrealistic will demotivate staff.

6 (a) Tasks should be allocated to the time available based on their **urgency** and their **importance**.

(b) Diaries and calendars can be physical documents or computer software.

True ✓

A calendar is the most appropriate tool for making sure that you do not forget to complete a task when you are busy.

False ✓

7 (a) Employees have a responsibility to report any health and safety risks in the workplace.

True ✓

(b) Employers have a responsibility to provide new staff with an induction that covers the organisation's policies and procedures.

True ✓

8   (a) Hybrid working is where employees decide how many hours they need to work each day.

   False ✓

   (b) Working collaboratively on a document store in the cloud is an example of shared communication channels.

   True ✓

9   (a) Locks on filing cabinets where paper copies of confidential documents are kept is an example of

   | **physical access restrictions** |

   (b) Software designed to prevent unauthorised access to a system by blocking intruders or malicious software at the point of entry into the system is

   | **a firewall** |

   (c) Encouraging victims to part with confidential information by sending emails from apparently trusted sources is known as hacking.

   False ✓

   (d) Using sophisticated software to guess passwords or find loopholes in security that they can exploit to gain access is known as phishing.

   False ✓

10 (a) (i) Total expenses = £197,583 + £285,900

   £ | 483,483 |

   (ii) Profit = £380,000 + £197,500 – £483,483

   £ | 94,017 |

   (b) Profit as a percentage of sales = £94,017 ÷ £577,500 × 100

   | 16.28 | %

11 Organisations have assets, liabilities, income and expenditure.

(a)

Description	Term described
Money spent by the organisation	Expenses
Money earned by the organisation	Income

(b)

Description	Term described
An amount paid to purchase motor insurance	Expense
A sale to a customer on credit	Income

12 When an organisation sells goods to a customer and the customer pays for the goods three weeks after the goods are delivered, this is known as a **credit sale.**

When an organisation buys services from a person and pays that person on the day the service is carried out, this is known as a **cash purchase.**

13 An organisation sends **an invoice** to a customer for goods sold for credit.

An organisation gets **a delivery note** from a supplier accompanying goods it receives.

An organisation receives **a purchase order** from a customer requesting that the goods specified in the document be sold to the customer.

14 (a)

Quantity supplied ✓

Customer order number ✓

(b)

Purchase order and goods received note ✓

Test your learning: answers

15 (a) 30 days after invoice date ✓

(b) Increasing the period of credit offered to customers ✓

16 This discrepancy should be identified by comparing the goods received note to the purchase order.

True ✓

17 (a) £ 2,176

(b) It will cause it to fall. ✓

(c) Customers will raise a query with General Retail if the quantity of goods recorded on a GRN doesn't match the amount ordered. ✓

Chapter 4

1. (a) The average price of each car = £958.30 ÷ 2

    £ **479.15**

   (b) £958.30 + £1,200 = £2,158.30

    £ **2,158.30**

   (c) (1,200 ÷ £2,158.30) × 100% = 56%

    56 %

2. (a) The increase in selling price for product number 52 = £17 × 1 ÷ 5

    £ **3.40**

   (b) The increase in selling price for product number 12 = £18 ÷ 100 × 6

    £ **1.08**

3. (a) The increase in selling price for product number 104 = £62 × 1 ÷ 10

    £ **6.20**

   (b) The increase in selling price for product number AZ25 = £9 ÷ 100 × 7.5

    £ **0.68**

4. (a) Sales at Outlet 4

Sales per outlet	£
Outlet 1	250,368.25
Outlet 2	199,473.79
Outlet 3	302,699.39
Outlet 4	**375,210.17**
Total	1,127,751.60

(b) Average sales per outlet = £1,127,751.60 ÷ 4

£ 281,937.90

(c) Sales from menswear

Item	£
Menswear	76,203
Ladieswear	61,506
Childrenswear	62,595
Household fabrics	50,076
Total	250,380

(d) The ratio of total sales at Outlet 1 to sales of childrenswear at Outlet 1

4:1

(e) The percentage that household fabrics is of the total sales at Outlet 1

50,076 ÷ 250,380 × 100 = 20%

5 (a) The costs at Premises 2

Costs per premises	£
Premises 1	50,924.72
Premises 2	51,125.22
Total	102,049.94

(b) Average cost per premises = £102,049.94 ÷ 2

£ 51,024.97

(c) The ratio of total costs to administration costs

5:1

(d) Express your answer to (c) as a percentage

1 ÷ 5 × 100 = 20 %

6 (a) Appropriate formula to calculate the total sales figure for January

=B3+C3 or =SUM(B3:C3)

(b) Appropriate formula to calculate the UK sales figure for February

=D4-C4

(c) Appropriate formula to calculate the total UK sales figure

=B3+B4 or =SUM(B3:B4)

(d) Appropriate formula to calculate the total UK and overseas sales figure

=D3+D4 or =SUM(D3:D4)

Or

=B5+C5 or =SUM(B5:C5)

(e) To change the background colour of a cell you should select this button.

The other buttons (in order of appearance) are to format in thousands, change the colour of the font and to underline the cell contents.

Practice assessments

Level 1 — Business Skills
BPP practice assessment 1

Task 1 [12 marks]

This task is about understanding organisation types, structures and sectors.

(a) Identify whether the following statements are true or false. (4 marks)

Statement	True	False
The fire service is a private sector organisation.		
A public limited company is in the public sector.		
A bank is in the services sector.		
An office cleaning company is in the retail sector.		

(b) Identify whether the following organisations are run for profit or not for profit. (4 marks)

Statement	For profit	Not for profit
Social enterprise		
Private limited company		
Partnership		
Voluntary organisation		

(c) Identify which function of a business relates to the following statements. (4 marks)

Statement	Department
Ensures raw materials are made into finished goods efficiently	Option 1
Interacts with customers	Option 2
Delivers finished goods to the customer	Option 3
Supports other business areas with systems to help them meet their objectives	Option 4

Options	Answer
Information technology	
Production	
Sales and marketing	
Distribution	

Task 2 [14 marks]

This task is about understanding how sales and purchases support businesses.

(a) Identify whether the following statements are true or false. (4 marks)

Statement	True	False
Losses do not affect a business' bank account.		
Sales with payment terms of 30 days will lead to a lower bank balance than cash sales.		
A higher proportion of payroll costs in total expenses will lead to a higher bank balance.		
If expenditure is less than sales then a loss is made.		

(b) Identify whether each of the items listed is an example of income or expenditure. (4 marks)

Statement	Income	Expenditure
Insurance		
Cash sale		
Loan interest		
Credit sale		

(c) Identify whether each of the following is a profit, surplus, loss or deficit. (4 marks)

Statement	Department
A social enterprise's expenses are less than its income.	Option 1
A public limited company's income is less than its expenses.	Option 2
A partnership's expenses are less than its income.	Option 3
A community interest company's expenses are more than its income.	Option 4

Options	Answer
Profit	
Surplus	
Loss	
Deficit	

(d) **Identify the date each of the following payments is due.** (2 marks)

Payment terms	Invoice Date	Payment due
At the end of the month of invoice	10th May	
14 days after the invoice date	28th May	

Options	Answer
24th May	
31st May	
11th June	
14th June	

Task 3 [12 marks]

This task is about understanding business procedures for sales, purchases and expenses.

(a) **Identify which ONE of the following documents is NOT prepared by the seller of goods in a credit transaction.** (1 mark)

Statement	Answer
Goods received note	
Goods despatched note	
Sales invoice	

(b) **Identify whether the following statements are true or false.** (4 marks)

Statement	True	False
Customers include payment terms on customer orders stating when they are prepared to pay.		
A service business such as a law firm usually refers to people using its services as customers.		
It is more important that documents related to sales are completed quickly than worrying about whether they are completely accurately.		
The details describing the goods on a delivery note and related goods received note would normally be expected to match.		

(c) **Complete the following statements.** (2 marks)

Statement	Gap	Statement
An organisation receives		from a supplier with goods supplied.
An organisation sends		to a supplier requesting that the goods specified in the document be sold to the organisation.

Gap 1	Answer
a delivery note	
a goods received note	
a purchase invoice	

Gap 2	Answer
a purchase invoice	
a delivery note	
a purchase order	

You have been asked to check the following invoice and delivery note.

INVOICE	Invoice number 56314
Best Components Ltd **Unit 13,** **New Industrial Park** **Port Town PT2 3FD** **Tel: 0178 2449888**	
VAT registration:	0123 2888 36
Date/tax point:	5 November 20XX
Order number:	02989
Customer:	HRD Electricals 347 High Street Lakewood LW1 7GG
Account number (customer code)	3422 H

Description/product code	Quantity	Unit amount £	Total £
LED displays	100	150.00	15,000.00
A7 Chipsets	200	42.50	8,500.00
USB ports	350	1.75	612.50
Net total			29,625.00
VAT at 20%			5,925.00
Invoice total			35,550.00
Terms 30 days			

GOODS RECEIVED NOTE						
Delivery from: **Best Components Ltd** **Unit 13,** **New Industrial Park** **Port Town PT2 3FD**				GRN Number:		00444
^				Supplier code:		2398
^				Order no:		02989
Date received:				7 December 20XX		
Account number (customer code)				3422 H		
Order no.	Desc.	Unit price	Units	Total Price (net)	VAT	Total Price (Gross)
32011	LED display	150.00	80	12,000.00	2,400.00	14,400.00
32011	A9 Chipset	42.50	200	8,500.00	1,700.00	10,200.00
32011	USB ports	1.75	350	612.50	122.50	735.00
Total			630	24,112.50	4,222.50	25,335.00
Received by: Martin Rigby						

(d) Identify whether the following statements are true or false. (5 marks)

Statement	True	False
The correct number of LED displays was invoiced.		
The incorrect chipset was invoiced.		
The correct unit price was invoiced for the USB ports.		
The invoice date is incorrect.		
There is a miscalculation in the total net amount.		

Task 4 [10 marks]

This task is about performing and checking simple calculations and formatting data to enhance the presentation of data.

Sales at Artim's Bakery for the last six months are provided in the spreadsheet below.

(a) (i) Identify the month with the highest sales by changing the cell fill colour. (2 marks)

(ii) Identify the lowest monthly sales figure by underlining it. (2 marks)

	A	B	C	D	E	F	G
1		Jul	Aug	Sept	Oct	Nov	Dec
2		£	£	£	£	£	£
3	Sales	4,446	3,209	4,599	2,990	2,766	8,846

(b) Using the data in part (a)

(i) Establish the range for monthly sales. (1 mark)

£ ☐

(ii) Calculate the mean monthly sales. (1 mark)

£ ☐

You have been asked to calculate the total monthly sales for the last quarter of the year.

(c) State how many months' figures this will include. (1 mark)

☐

You have been given the following spreadsheet that shows cash and credit card receipts at a large shop.

	A	B	C	D
1	Day	Cash receipts	Credit card receipts	Total receipts
2		£	£	£
3	1	2687	12357	15044
4	2	2415	16974	18649
5	3	3675	21874	25549
6	4	5473	10478	15951

(d) (i) Format the figures in B3:D6 as thousands. (1 mark)

Column D shows the total of cash and credit card receipts each day. You have been asked to check that the totals have been calculated correctly.

(ii) Change the fill colour in column D where the total has been added up incorrectly. (2 marks)

Task 5 [16 marks]

This task is about performing more complex calculations and using simple formulas.

(a) Complete the table below to express figures as percentages, fractions and decimals. (4 marks)

Percentage	Fraction	Decimal
75%		
		0.1

(b) Record 4/5 as a decimal. (1 mark)

You have been provided with the following analysis of daily takings from cash sales to be paid into Tricky Traders' bank account:

Four	£50 notes
Two	£20 notes
Four	£5 note
Twenty	50 pence coins
Fifteen	20 pence coins

(c) Using the information provided, complete the following calculations. (3 marks)

Calculation	Answer
What is the total amount that will be paid into the bank account?	
What percentage of the total amount is made up of £5 notes? Round your answer to two decimal places.	
What is the ratio of the number of notes to the number of coins?	

You have been provided with the following partially completed spreadsheet showing sales in the North and South regions of an organisation.

(d) (i) Use an appropriate formula in cell D3 to show total sales for September.
(2 marks)

(ii) Use an appropriate formula in cell B4 to show North's sales for October.
(2 marks)

(iii) Use an appropriate formula in cell C5 to show South's sales for November.
(2 marks)

(iv) Use an appropriate formula in cell D6 to show total sales for September, October and November.
(2 marks)

	A	B	C	D
1	Month	North Sales	South Sales	Total sales
2		£	£	£
3	September	6,475	8,745	
4	October		4,215	8,418
5	November	5,476		12,932
6	Total sales	16,154	20,416	
7				

Task 6 [16 marks]

This task is about developing skills for the workplace.

You have been asked to draft an email to the finance director of your organisation, requesting that they approve the payment of some invoices for you. You are now checking the email before you send it. The finance director's name is Jasmine Brogan and you have never met her.

> To Jaz
>
> I need you to approve the attached invoices as soon as possible so we can pay them.
>
> If you have any questions then give me a shout.
>
> Lenny
>
> Accounts Assistant
>
> 01234 567890
>
> L+G Ltd

(a) (i) Identify whether the following statements are true or false. (3 marks)

Statement	True	False
The email addresses the finance director appropriately.		
There are no spelling errors in the email.		
The email is written politely.		

(ii) Identify whether the following statement is true or false. (1 mark)

Statement	True	False
It is appropriate to use an email to request approval of the invoices.		

(b) Identify the most appropriate method of communication in each of the following circumstances. (4 marks)

Statement	Department
To formally request payment for an overdue invoice	Option 1
To investigate why a customer has not paid the correct amount owed	Option 2
To collaborate on a shared presentation document	Option 3
To share company policy and procedure documents	Option 4

Options	Answer
Shared communication channel	
Letter	
Instant message	
Telephone	
Intranet	

(c) Identify whether the following actions are acceptable or unacceptable in the workplace. (4 marks)

Statement	Acceptable	Unacceptable
Leaving work early with the approval of your manager		
Having your personal phone on your desk so you can keep up-to-date with social media messages		
Speaking over people in meetings to get your message across		
Telling your colleagues if you are struggling to meet their deadlines		

Jamal, a new employee at David's Sock Suppliers Ltd, has to choose a password to enable access to the company's computer systems.

(d) (i) The primary reason for this is best described by which ONE of the following?
(1 mark)

Statement	Answer
Information and data security	
Confidentiality	
Work scheduling	

(ii) Which of the following would be the most effective password for Jamal to select? (1 mark)

Statement	Answer
Computer	
12345	
J@ma1	

David's Sock Supplies Ltd wishes to increase its data and information security in order to enable the company to recover its data if it were damaged or destroyed.

(e) Which of the following would be the most appropriate action to achieve this objective? (1 mark)

Statement	Answer
Install anti-virus software on the IT system	
Introduce back-up procedures	
Put in place restrictions on physical access	

David's Sock Supplies Ltd has recently had confidential emails intercepted while they were being sent to the recipient.

(f) Which of the following data security methods could have prevented this? (1 mark)

Statement	Answer
Firewall	
Anti-virus software	
Encryption	

Level 1 — Business Skills
BPP practice assessment 1: answers

Task 1

(a) **Identify whether the following statements are true or false.** (4 marks)

Statement	True	False
The fire service is a private sector organisation.		✓
A public limited company is in the public sector.		✓
A bank is in the services sector.	✓	
An office cleaning company is in the retail sector.		✓

(b) **Identify whether the following organisations are run for profit or not for profit.** (4 marks)

Statement	For profit	Not for profit
Social enterprise		✓
Private limited company	✓	
Partnership	✓	
Voluntary organisation		✓

(c) **Identify which function of a business relates to the following statements.** (4 marks)

Statement	Department
Ensures raw materials are made into finished goods efficiently	Production
Interacts with customers	Sales and marketing
Delivers finished goods to the customer	Distribution
Supports other business areas with systems to help them meet their objectives	Information technology

Task 2

(a) Identify whether the following statements are true or false. **(4 marks)**

Statement	True	False
Losses do not affect a business' bank account.		✓
Sales with payment terms of 30 days will lead to a lower bank balance than cash sales.	✓	
A higher proportion of payroll costs in total expenses will lead to a higher bank balance.		✓
If expenditure is less than sales then a loss is made.		✓

(b) Identify whether each of the items listed is an example of income or expenditure. **(4 marks)**

Statement	Income	Expenditure
Insurance		✓
Cash sale	✓	
Loan interest		✓
Credit sale	✓	

(c) Identify whether each of the following is a profit, surplus, loss or deficit. **(4 marks)**

Statement	Department
A social enterprise's expenses are less than its income.	Surplus
A public limited company's income is less than its expenses.	Loss
A partnership's expenses are less than its income.	Profit
A community interest company's expenses are more than its income.	Deficit

(d) Identify the date each of the following payments is due. **(2 marks)**

Payment terms	Invoice Date	Payment due
At the end of the month of invoice	10th May	31st May
14 days after the invoice date	28th May	11th June

Task 3

(a) Identify which ONE of the following documents is NOT prepared by the seller of goods in a credit transaction. (1 mark)

Statement	Answer
Goods received note	✓
Goods despatched note	
Sales invoice	

(b) Identify whether the following statements are true or false. (4 marks)

Statement	True	False
Customers include payment terms on customer orders stating when they are prepared to pay.		✓
A service business such as a law firm usually refers to people using its services as customers.		✓
It is more important that documents related to sales are completed quickly than worrying about whether they are completely accurately.		✓
The details describing the goods on a delivery note and related goods received note would normally be expected to match.	✓	

(c) Complete the following statements. (2 marks)

Statement	Gap	Statement
An organisation receives	a delivery note	from a supplier with goods supplied.
An organisation sends	a purchase order	to a supplier requesting that the goods specified in the document be sold to the organisation.

(d) Identify whether the following statements are true or false. (5 marks)

Statement	True	False
The correct number of LED displays was invoiced.		✓
The incorrect chipset was invoiced.	✓	
The correct unit price was invoiced for the USB ports.	✓	
The invoice date is incorrect.		✓
There is a miscalculation in the total net amount.	✓	

Task 4

(a) (i) Identify the month with the highest sales by changing the cell fill colour. (2 marks)

(ii) Identify the lowest monthly sales figure by underlining it. (2 marks)

	A	B	C	D	E	F	G
1		Jul	Aug	Sept	Oct	Nov	Dec
2		£	£	£	£	£	£
3	Sales	4,446	3,209	4,599	2,990	<u>2,766</u>	8,846

(b) Using the data in part (a)

(i) Establish the range for monthly sales. (1 mark)

£ | 6,080 |

(ii) Calculate the mean monthly sales. (1 mark)

£ | 4,476 |

(c) State how many months' figures this will include. (1 mark)

| 3 |

(d) (i) Format the figures in B3:D6 as thousands. (1 mark)

(ii) Change the fill colour in column D where the total has been added up incorrectly. (2 marks)

	A	B	C	D
1	Day	Cash receipts	Credit card receipts	Total receipts
2		£	£	£
3	1	2,687	12,357	15,044
4	2	2,415	16,974	18,649
5	3	3,675	21,874	25,549
6	4	5,473	10,478	15,951

Task 5

(a) Complete the table below to express figures as percentages, fractions and decimals. (4 marks)

Percentage	Fraction	Decimal
75%	3/4	0.75
10%	1/10	0.1

(b) Record 4/5 as a decimal. (1 mark)

0.8

(c) Using the information provided, complete the following calculations. (3 marks)

Calculation	Answer
What is the total amount that will be paid into the bank account?	273
What percentage of the total amount is made up of £5 notes? Round your answer to two decimal places.	7.33
What is the ratio of the number of notes to the number of coins?	2:7

(d) (i) Use an appropriate formula in cell D3 to show total sales for September. (2 marks)

    (ii) Use an appropriate formula in cell B4 to show North's sales for October. (2 marks)

    (iii) Use an appropriate formula in cell C5 to show South's sales for November. (2 marks)

    (iv) Use an appropriate formula in cell D6 to show total sales for September, October and November. (2 marks)

	A	B	C	D
1	Month	North Sales	South Sales	Total sales
2		£	£	£
3	September	6,475		8,745	15,220
4	October	4,203	4,215	8,418
5	November	5,476	7,456	12,932
6	Total sales	16,154	20,416	36,570

Formula:

D4 =sum(B3:C3) or =B3+C3

B4 =D4-C4

C5 =D5-B5

D6 =sum(B6:C6) or =B6+C6 or =sum(D3:D5) or =D3+D4+D5

Task 6

(a) (i) Identify whether the following statements are true or false. **(3 marks)**

Statement	True	False
The email addresses the finance director appropriately.		✓
There are no spelling errors in the email.		✓
The email is written politely.		✓

(ii) Identify whether the following statement is true or false. **(1 mark)**

Statement	True	False
It is appropriate to use an email to request approval of the invoices.	✓	

(b) Identify the most appropriate method of communication in each of the following circumstances. **(4 marks)**

Statement	Department
To formally request payment for an overdue invoice	Letter
To investigate why a customer has not paid the correct amount owed	Telephone
To collaborate on a shared presentation document	Shared communication channel
To share company policy and procedure documents	Intranet

(c) Identify whether the following actions are acceptable or unacceptable in the workplace. **(4 marks)**

Statement	Acceptable	Unacceptable
Leaving work early with the approval of your manager	✓	
Having your personal phone on your desk so you can keep up-to-date with social media messages		✓
Speaking over people in meetings to get your message across		✓
Telling your colleagues if you are struggling to meet their deadlines	✓	

(d) (i) The primary reason for this is best described by which ONE of the following? **(1 mark)**

Statement	Answer
Information and data security	✓
Confidentiality	
Work scheduling	

(ii) Which of the following would be the most effective password for Jamal to select? (1 mark)

Statement	Answer
Computer	
12345	
J@ma1	✓

(e) Which of the following would be the most appropriate action to achieve this objective? (1 mark)

Statement	Answer
Install anti-virus software on the IT system	
Introduce back-up procedures	✓
Put in place restrictions on physical access	

(f) Which of the following data security methods could have prevented this? (1 mark)

Statement	Answer
Firewall	
Anti-virus software	
Encryption	✓

Level 1 — Business Skills
BPP practice assessment 2

Task 1 [12 marks]

This task is about understanding organisation types, structures and sectors.

(a) Identify whether the following statements are true or false. (4 marks)

Statement	True	False
Private limited companies cannot sell their shares on a stock market.		
In a partnership there is no legal distinction between the business and the partners who run it.		
Sole traders are run to make a profit.		
Public limited companies are funded by the government.		

(b) Identify whether the following statements are true or false. (4 marks)

Statement	True	False
The size of an organisation will not influence how it is structured.		
There is no legal requirement for organisations to act sustainably.		
In an organisation, employees are not required to have access to the same opportunities and benefits.		
Community interest companies are not run to make a profit.		

(c) Identify which sector relates to the following statements. (4 marks)

Statement	Department
The purpose is to achieve government objectives	Option 1
Income supports specified purpose	Option 2
Produces finished goods	Option 3
Sells finished goods to the public	Option 4

Sector	Answer
Voluntary sector	
Retail sector	
Public sector	
Services sector	
Manufacturing sector	

Task 2 [14 mark]

This task is about understanding how sales and purchases support businesses.

(a) **Identify whether the following statements are true or false.** (4 marks)

Statement	True	False
Not-for-profit organisations make a loss if income exceeds expenditure.		
For-profit organisations suffer a deficit if expenditure exceeds income.		
Not-for-profit organisations cannot make a profit or deficit.		
Both for-profit and not-for-profit organisations will suffer an outflow of money if their expenditure exceeds income.		

(b) **Identify whether each of the items listed is an example of an income or expenditure.** (4 marks)

Statement	Income	Expenditure
Bank interest received		
Goods purchased for resale		
Sales paid for immediately		
Sales paid 10 days after invoice date		

(c) **Identify whether the following statements are true or false.** (4 marks)

Statement	True	False
Making a distribution to the business' owners is one use for the organisation's profit.		
Cash paid into a bank from the sale of goods will affect the bank balance today.		
Making losses cannot cause a business to become overdrawn on its bank account.		
Sales made on credit terms will affect the bank balance on the day the sale is made.		

(d) Identify the date each of the following payments are due. (2 marks)

Payment terms	Invoice Date	Payment due
At the end of the month of invoice	13th October	
7 days after the invoice date	23rd September	

Options	Answer
20th September	
30th September	
30th October	
31st October	

Task 3 [12 marks]

This task is about understanding business procedures for sales, purchases and expenses.

You work for Acme Trading as a purchase order clerk. You have been asked to place an order for 14 office chairs.

(a) What would be the best procedure for finding a supplier? (1 mark)

Statement	Answer
Ask a friend to recommend a supplier	
Use Acme Trading's approved supplier list	
Use an internet search engine	

(b) Identify whether the following statements are true or false. (4 marks)

Statement	True	False
The date on an invoice should be the day the customer order was received.		
Organisations use standardised procedures and documents for sales and purchases to improve efficiency and save time.		
The format of documents for sales and purchases is set out by law.		
Finished goods made by a business are sold to customers.		

(c) **Complete the following statements.** (2 marks)

Statement	Gap	Statement
An organisation provides		to a customer when it supplies goods ordered.
An organisation sends		to a customer listing goods sold to the customer and showing the amount due to be paid, and when it is due to be paid.

Gap 1	Answer
a delivery note	
a goods received note	
a sales invoice	

Gap 2	Answer
a sales invoice	
a delivery note	
a purchase order	

You have been asked to check the following delivery note and goods received note.

DELIVERY NOTE	Delivery note number 7845
Bland Supplies Ltd **Unit 31,** **Kings Industrial Estate** **Newtown NT1 3TP** **Tel: 01307 648756**	
VAT registration:	0123 4777 22
Date/tax point:	7 April 20XX
Order number:	02989
Customer:	Mount Lemond Ltd 123 London Road Gazeborough GB7 8UU
Account number (customer code)	4421 B

Description/product code	Quantity	Unit amount £	Total £
Flash Mountings	90	100.00	9,000.00
Bespoke Roundings	150	32.75	4,912.50
Grated Chippings	2,000	3.25	6,500 00
Net total			20,412.50
VAT at 20%			5,103.13
Invoice total			25,515.63
Terms 30 days			

GOODS RECEIVED NOTE

Delivery from: **Bland Supplies Ltd** Unit 31, Kings Industrial Estate Newtown NT1 3TP Tel: 01307 648756			GRN Number:		00444		
			Supplier code:		2398		
			Delivery note no:		7845		
		Date received:	9 August 20XX				
Account number (customer code)			4421 B				
Order no.	Desc.	Unit price	Units	Total Price (net)	VAT	Total Price (Gross)
2022	Flash Mountings	100.00	90	9,000.00	2,250.00	11,250.00
2022	Bespoke Roundings	32.75	125	4,093.75	1,023.44	5,117,19
2022	Grated Chippings	3.25	2,000	6,500.00	1,625.00	8,125.00
Total			2,215	19,593.75	4,898.54	24,492.19
		Received by: Jo Spence				

(d) Identify whether the following statements are true or false. (5 marks)

Statement	True	False
The goods received note refers to the correct order number		
The dates on the documents are consistent with each other		
There are no calculation errors on the goods received note		
The full quantity of goods ordered was delivered		
The goods received note should have been signed		

Task 4 [10 marks]

This task is about performing and checking simple calculations and formatting data to enhance the presentation of data.

Details of employee expenses for a travel agent are provided in the spreadsheet below.

(a) (i) Identify the month with the highest expenses by changing the font colour.

(2 marks)

(ii) Identify the lowest monthly expenses figure by making it bold. (2 marks)

	A	B
1	Month	Expenses
2		£
3	January	5,423
4	February	4,875
5	March	6,321
6	April	7,452
7	May	2,153
8	June	2,036
9	July	3,695
10	August	9,965
11	September	9,969
12	October	5,412
13	November	3,258
14	December	2,247

(b) **Using the data in part (a)**

(i) Calculate the increase in expenses between June and July. (1 mark)

£ [ ]

(ii) Calculate the average (mean) expenses for January, February and March.

(1 mark)

£ [ ]

You have been asked to rank the expenses for October, November and December in ascending order.

(c) **State the month that would appear first in the ranking.** (1 mark)

[ ]

(d) **Match the number in words to the numbers in figures.** (3 marks)

Statement	Answer
Two hundred and five pounds and fifty pence	Option 1
Two hundred and fifty pounds	Option 2
Two hundred pounds and twenty-five pence	Option 3

Options	Answer
£250.00	
£205.50	
£200.25	

Task 5 [16 marks]

This task is about performing more complex calculations and using simple formulae.

(a) **Complete the following calculations.** (4 marks)

Statement	Answer
Show 1/10 as a percentage.	Option 1
Show 30 minutes as a percentage of an hour.	Option 2
State 4/5 as a decimal.	
State 0.04 as a percentage.	

Options	Answer
1%	
10%	
30%	
50%	

(b) **Complete the following calculations, stating your answer to two decimal places.**

(2 marks)

Calculation	Answer
A product normally sells for £15; during a sale it is sold at 25% off. Calculate the sale price of the product.	
The normal selling price of a product is £21, the business now wishes to increase the selling price by 15%. Calculate the amount of the increase.	

The following information is available regarding the number of stationery products sold last month.

Product	Sales
Pens	2,236
Rubbers	3,575
Elastic bands	559
Staples	7,150

(c) **Complete the following ratios.** (2 marks)

Description	Ratio
Elastic bands to pens	
Rubbers to staples	

You have been provided with the following partially completed spreadsheet showing sales, income, expenses and profit for an organisation. Expenses cost £3 per unit sold.

(d) (i) **Use an appropriate formula in cell E3 to show profit for January.** (2 marks)

(ii) **Use an appropriate formula in cell B4 to show sales for February.** (2 marks)

(iii) **Use an appropriate formula in cell C5 to show income for March.** (2 marks)

(iv) **Use an appropriate formula in cell E6 to show profit for January, February and March.** (2 marks)

	A	B	C	D	E
1	Month	Sales (units)	Income	Expenses	Profit
2			£	£	
3	January	500	2,000	1,500	
4	February		1,500	1,125	375
5	March	650		1,950	650
6					
7					

Task 6 [16 marks]

This task is about developing skills for the workplace.

You have been asked to send an application pack to someone enquiring after a job in your organisation.

(a) **Select the most appropriate form of communication to accompany the application pack.** (1 mark)

Form of communication	Answer
Letter	
Spreadsheet	
Report	

It is important to observe confidentiality.

(b) **Complete the following sentences by inserting the most appropriate option from the lists below.** (2 marks)

Statement	Answer
Chandra is working on the payroll. She leaves her desk to make a cup of tea. She should:	Option 1
A friend is a journalist, writing a story on local businesses for the local paper. She asks you how many people your organisation employs. You reply:	Option 2

Option 1	Answer
Leave the payroll documents on her desk, as she'll only be gone five minutes.	
Lock the payroll documents in her desk drawer, because she will be away from her desk.	

Option 2	Answer
'200.'	
'I don't think it is appropriate for you to ask me; you should contact the managing director.'	

(c) Identify whether the following statements are true or false. (4 marks)

Statement	True	False
Regular use of social media to communicate with friends while at work is acceptable because it will not disturb co-workers.		
The person who sets your goals at work and monitors your performance is determined by the organisation's reporting lines.		
Whether you meet your deadlines or not will affect others.		
The urgency of the work is the only factor to consider when prioritising your work.		

(d) (Identify whether the following statements are true or false. (4 marks)

Statement	True	False
It is important to share computers as this protects against lost data.		
Back-ups of data should be stored close to the system in case they are needed quickly.		
Screensavers help protect the security of a computer.		
Anti-virus software should be installed on all computers.		

(e) Identify whether the following statement is true or false. (1 mark)

Statement	True	False
It is the responsibility of employees to report any health and safety risks they find in the workplace.		

You have been asked to draft a letter to the finance director of a customer, requesting that they pay for some goods. Payment was due a month ago and you do not know the name of the finance director. You are now checking the letter before you send it.

> Elsie May
> DP Products Ltd
> 15 Faith Street
> Mazeborough
> M5 7YU
>
> The finance director
> PJK Ltd
> 140 Rank Road
> Midhaven
> M1 4ET
>
>
> Dear Sirs
>
> It has come to my attention that we have not yet received payment for goods that we delivered to your company on 15th May 20XX.
>
> I would be grateful if you could look into this and forward payment for the goods within the next week or we may consider taking legal action to recover the money owed to us.
>
> Please do not hesitate to contact me if you have any queries.
>
> Elsie May
> Accounts assistant
> 01267 569754
> DP Products Ltd

(f) Identify whether the following statements are true or false. (4 marks)

Statement	True	False
The letter addresses the finance director appropriately.		
There are no spelling errors in the email.		
The email is written politely.		
The letter contains all the information the finance director needs to respond.		

Level 1 — Business Skills
BPP practice assessment 2: answers

Task 1

(a) Identify whether the following statements are true or false. (4 marks)

Statement	True	False
Private limited companies cannot sell their shares on a stock market.	✓	
In a partnership there is no legal distinction between the business and the partners who run it.	✓	
Sole traders are run to make a profit.	✓	
Public limited companies are funded by the government.		✓

(b) Identify whether the following statements are true or false. (4 marks)

Statement	True	False
The size of an organisation will not influence how it is structured.		✓
There is no legal requirement for organisations to act sustainably.	✓	
In an organisation, employees are not required to have access to the same opportunities and benefits.		✓
Community interest companies are not run to make a profit.	✓	

(c) Identify which sector relates to the following statements. (4 marks)

Statement	Department
The purpose is to achieve government objectives	Public sector
Income supports specified purpose	Voluntary sector
Produces finished goods	Manufacturing sector
Sells finished goods to the public	Retail sector

Task 2

(a) Identify whether the following statements are true or false. (4 marks)

Statement	True	False
Not-for-profit organisations make a loss if income exceeds expenditure.		✓
For-profit organisations suffer a deficit if expenditure exceeds income.		✓
Not-for-profit organisations cannot make a profit or deficit.		✓
Both for-profit and not-for-profit organisations will suffer an outflow of money if their expenditure exceeds income.	✓	

(b) Identify whether each of the items listed is an example of an income or expenditure. (4 marks)

Statement	Income	Expenditure
Bank interest received	✓	
Goods purchased for resale		✓
Sales paid for immediately	✓	
Sales paid 10 days after invoice date	✓	

(c) Identify whether the following statements are true or false. (4 marks)

Statement	True	False
Making a distribution to the business' owners is one use for the organisation's profit.	✓	
Cash paid into a bank from the sale of goods will affect the bank balance today.	✓	
Making losses cannot cause a business to become overdrawn on its bank account.		✓
Sales made on credit terms will affect the bank balance on the day the sale is made.		✓

(d) Identify the date each of the following payments are due. (2 marks)

Payment terms	Invoice Date	Payment due
At the end of the month of invoice	13th October	31st October
7 days after the invoice date	23rd September	30th September

Task 3

(a) What would be the best procedure for finding a supplier? (1 mark)

Statement	Answer
Ask a friend to recommend a supplier	
Use Acme Trading's approved supplier list	✓
Use an internet search engine	

(b) Identify whether the following statements are true or false. (4 marks)

Statement	True	False
The date on an invoice should be the day the customer order was received.		✓
Organisations use standardised procedures and documents for sales and purchases to improve efficiency and save time.	✓	
The format of documents for sales and purchases is set out by law.		✓
Finished goods made by a business are sold to customers.	✓	

(c) Complete the following statements. (2 marks)

Statement	Gap	Statement
An organisation provides	a delivery note	to a customer when it supplies goods ordered.
An organisation sends	a sales invoice	to a customer listing goods sold to the customer and showing the amount due to be paid, and when it is due to be paid.

(d) Identify whether the following statements are true or false. (5 marks)

Statement	True	False
The goods received note refers to the correct order number		✓
The dates on the documents are consistent with each other		✓
There are no calculation errors on the goods received note	✓	
The full quantity of goods ordered was delivered		✓
The goods received note should have been signed	✓	

Task 4

(a) (i) Identify the month with the highest expenses by changing the font colour. (2 marks)

(ii) Identify the lowest monthly expenses figure by making it bold. (2 marks)

	A	B
1	Month	Expenses
2		£
3	January	5,423
4	February	4,875
5	March	6,321
6	April	7,452
7	May	2,153
8	June	**2,036**
9	July	3,695
10	August	9,965
11	September	9,969
12	October	5,412
13	November	3,258
14	December	2,247

(b) Using the data in part (a)

(i) Calculate the increase in expenses between June and July. (1 mark)

£ 1,659

(ii) Calculate the average (mean) expenses for January, February and March. (1 mark)

£ 5,540

(c) State the month that would appear first in the ranking. (1 mark)

December

(d) Match the number in words to the numbers in figures. (3 marks)

Statement	Answer
Two hundred and five pounds and fifty pence	£205.50
Two hundred and fifty pounds	£250.00
Two hundred pounds and twenty-five pence	£200.25

Task 5

(a) **Complete the following calculations.** (4 marks)

Statement	Answer
Show 1/10 as a percentage.	10%
Show 30 minutes as a percentage of an hour.	50%
State 4/5 as a decimal.	0.8
State 0.04 as a percentage.	4%

(b) **Complete the following calculations, stating your answer to two decimal places.** (2 marks)

Calculation	Answer
A product normally sells for £15; during a sale it is sold at 25% off. Calculate the sale price of the product.	£11.25
The normal selling price of a product is £21, the business now wishes to increase the selling price by 15%. Calculate the amount of the increase.	£3.15

(c) **Complete the following ratios.** (2 marks)

Description	Ratio
Elastic bands to pens	1:4
Rubbers to staples	2:1

(d) (i) Use an appropriate formula in cell E3 to show profit for January. (2 marks)

(ii) Use an appropriate formula in cell B4 to show sales for February. (2 marks)

(iii) Use an appropriate formula in cell C5 to show income for March. (2 marks)

(iv) Use an appropriate formula in cell E6 to show profit for January, February and March. (2 marks)

	A	B	C	D	E
1	Month	Sales (units)	Income	Expenses	Profit
2			£	£	
3	January	500	2,000	1,500	500
4	February	375	1,500	1,125	375
5	March	650	2,600	1,950	650
6					1,525

Formula:

E3 =C3-D3

B4 =D4/3

C5 =D5+E5

E6 =sum(E3:E5) or =E3+E4+E5

Task 6

(a) **Select the most appropriate form of communication to accompany the application pack.** (1 mark)

Form of communication	Answer
Letter	✓
Spreadsheet	
Report	

It is important to observe confidentiality.

(b) **Complete the following sentences by inserting the most appropriate option from the lists below.** (2 m

Statement	Answer
Chandra is working on the payroll. She leaves her desk to make a cup of tea. She should:	Lock the payroll documents in her desk drawer, because she will be away from her desk.
A friend is a journalist, writing a story on local businesses for the local paper. She asks you how many people your organisation employs. You reply:	'I don't think it is appropriate for you to ask me; you should contact the managing director.'

(c) **Identify whether the following statements are true or false.** (4 marks)

Statement	True	False
Regular use of social media to communicate with friends while at work is acceptable because it will not disturb co-workers.		✓
The person who sets your goals at work and monitors your performance is determined by the organisation's reporting lines.	✓	
Whether you meet your deadlines or not will affect others.	✓	
The urgency of the work is the only factor to consider when prioritising your work.		✓

(d) (Identify whether the following statements are true or false. (4 marks)

Statement	True	False
It is important to share computers as this protects against lost data.		✓
Back-ups of data should be stored close to the system in case they are needed quickly.		✓
Screensavers help protect the security of a computer.	✓	
Anti-virus software should be installed on all computers.	✓	

(e) Identify whether the following statement is true or false. (1 mark)

Statement	True	False
It is the responsibility of employees to report any health and safety risks they find in the workplace.	✓	

(f) Identify whether the following statements are true or false. (4 marks)

Statement	True	False
The letter addresses the finance director appropriately.	✓	
There are no spelling errors in the email.	✓	
The email is written politely.	✓	
The letter contains all the information the finance director needs to respond.		✓

Index

Access restrictions, 24
Accidental deletion, 26
Achieving goals, 11
Adaptability, 18
Addition, 65
Answering the phone, 17
Anti-virus software, 24
Authentication to access cloud-based information, 24
Averages, 78, 82

Back-ups, 23
Business procedures for purchases, 39
Business procedures for sales, 38

Calculator, 65
Cash and credit sales, 32
Cash purchase, 33
Cash sale, 32
Charities, 3, **4**, 5
Checklists, 14
Clear roles and responsibilities, 11
Client, 32
Collaboration, 10
Commitment, 18
Common goals, 12
Communication skills, 12
Community and voluntary organisations, 3, 4
Community Interest Companies (CICs), 3, 4
Confidentiality, 16, **21**, 22
Consequences of making losses, 30
Cookies and privacy settings, 24
Co-operation, 11
Corrupt files, 26
Credit purchase, 33
Credit sale, 32
Customer, 32
Customer order, 38, **40**

Data Protection Act, 16
Decimal, 72
Decimals, 77
Deficit, 27

Delivery note, 38, 39, **40**, 43
Denominator, 72
Departmental structure, 7
Developing workplace skills, 9
Diaries, 14
Distribution (despatch), 7
Diversity and equal opportunities, 4
Division, 67
Dress code, 17

Email, 19
Employee fraud, 26
Encryption, 23
Ethics, 4
Expenditure, 26
Expenses, 30

Face-to-face, 19
Factor, 72
Finance, 7
Firewalls, 23
Formatting the contents of spreadsheet cells, 83
Formulas, 82
Fraction, 72
Fractions, 71, 76, 77

General Data Protection Regulations, 16
Goods received note (GRN), 40

Hacking, 25
Honesty, 18
Human resources, 7
Hybrid working, 20

Importance, 15
Income, 26, **30**
Increases and decreases, 63
Information security, 21
Information technology (IT), 7
Instant messaging, 19
Intranet, 20
Invoice, 40

Index

Leadership, 11
Letter, 19
Limited Company, 2
Loss, 27

Manufacturing, 5
Mean, 79
Meeting deadlines, 13
Mode, 80
Multiplication, 67

Natural disasters, 26
Not sharing computers, 24
Numerator, 72

Online calendars, 14
Online collaboration, 14
Online meetings, 20
Opportunities from making a profit, 30
Order, 42
Organisation chart, 9
Organisational reporting lines, 8

Partnerships, 2
Passwords, 23
Payment terms, 33
Percentages, 74, 77
Personal qualities, 18
Phishing, 25
Policies and procedures, 10
Polite communication, 17
Prioritising tasks, 15
Private limited company (Ltd), 2
Private sector, 4
Production, 7
Professional behaviour, 16
Professionalism, 12
Profit, 27
Profit and loss, 26
Proportions, 71
Public limited company (PLC), 2
Public sector, 3, 4, 5
Purchase invoice, 39, 40
Purchase order, 39, 40
Purchases, 32

Range, 63
Range, 63
Ranking numbers, 61
Ratios, 70
Realistic deadlines, 12
Reliability, 12
Reporting lines, 8, 9
Reports, 19
Respect, 11
Responsibilities of the employee and employer, 10
Retail, 5
Rounding, 64
Rounding rule, 64
Rounding up, 67

Sales, 32
Sales and marketing, 7
Sales invoice, 38, 40
Screensavers, 23
Sectors, 5
Secure networks, 23
Securing confidential information, 24
Services, 5
Shared communication channels, 20
Shared learning, 11
Sharing ideas, 10
Social enterprises, 3, 4
Sole trader, 2
Spreadsheets, 20, 82
Structure, 9
Subtraction, 65
Supplier, 33
Surplus, 27
Surplus and deficit, 26
Sustainability, 4, 16
System crashes, 25

Team morale, 10
Team working, 11
Telephone, 19
Time, 69
Time management, 13
Time management tools, 14
Timekeeping, 12, 17
To-do lists, 14
Trust, 11

Trustworthiness, 18

Urgency, 15
Use of personal phones, 16
Use of social media, 16
Utilising individuals' skills and expertise, 11

Viruses, 25

Work schedule, 14
Working with others, 10
Workplace communication, 19

AAT ACCESS AWARD IN BUSINESS SKILLS – LEVEL 1 WORKBOOK (2022/23)

REVIEW FORM

How have you used this Workbook?
(Tick one box only)

☐ Home study
☐ On a course _____
☐ Other _____

Why did you decide to purchase this Workbook? *(Tick one box only)*

☐ Have used BPP Workbooks in the past
☐ Recommendation by friend/colleague
☐ Recommendation by a college lecturer
☐ Saw advertising
☐ Other _____

During the past six months do you recall seeing/receiving either of the following?
(Tick as many boxes as are relevant)

☐ Our advertisement in *Accounting Technician*
☐ Our Publishing Catalogue

Which (if any) aspects of our advertising do you think are useful?
(Tick as many boxes as are relevant)

☐ Prices and publication dates of new editions
☐ Information on Workbook content
☐ Details of our free online offering
☐ None of the above

Your ratings, comments and suggestions would be appreciated on the following areas of this Workbook.

	Very useful	Useful	Not useful
Introduction	☐	☐	☐
Quality of explanations	☐	☐	☐
How it works	☐	☐	☐
Chapter tasks	☐	☐	☐
Chapter overviews	☐	☐	☐
Test your learning	☐	☐	☐
Keywords	☐	☐	☐
BPP practice assessments	☐	☐	☐
Index	☐	☐	☐

	Excellent	Good	Adequate	Poor
Overall opinion of this Workbook	☐	☐	☐	☐

Do you intend to continue using BPP Products?   ☐ Yes   ☐ No

Please note any further comments and suggestions/errors on the reverse of this page.

The BPP author of this edition can be emailed at: learningmedia@bpp.com

REVIEW FORM (continued)

TELL US WHAT YOU THINK

Please note any further comments and suggestions/errors below.